Careers in Focus

PUBLIC RELATIONS

Ferguson
An imprint of Infobase Publishing

Careers in Focus: Public Relations

Copyright © 2007 by Infobase Publishing

Ferguson
An imprint of Infobase Publishing
132 West 31st Street
New York NY 10001

Library of Congress Cataloging-in-Publication Data

Careers in focus : Public relations.
    p. cm.
  Includes index.
  ISBN-13: 978-0-8160-6574-5
  ISBN-10: 0-8160-6574-8
  1. Public relations--Vocational guidance--Juvenile literature. 2. Public relations--United States--Juvenile literature. I. J.G. Ferguson Publishing Company. II. Title: Public relations.
  HD59.C365 2007
  659.2023'73--dc22
                            2007005370

Ferguson books are available at special discounts when purchased in bulk quantities for businesses, associations, institutions, or sales promotions. Please call our Special Sales Department in New York at (212) 967-8800 or (800) 322-8755.

You can find Ferguson on the World Wide Web at http://www.fergpubco.com

Text design by David Strelecky
Cover design by Salvatore Luongo

Printed in the United States of America
MP MSRF 10 9 8 7 6 5 4 3 2 1

This book is printed on acid-free paper.

Table of Contents

Introduction

The origins of public relations date back to early Greece, when Socrates, Plato, and Aristotle developed rules of rhetoric that made arguments more effective. Their methods were used in jury trials, ethics instruction, and other situations in which reason guided the discussion.

Today, public relations professionals are employed by all sorts of publicity-conscious people and companies. Politicians, celebrities, artists, and even journalists now use specialists to help them receive positive coverage in the press. Public relations today is a major service industry, expanding beyond the original clients—business and government—to a whole range of clients who wish to put their best foot forward in their presentation to the public.

Approximately 425,000 full-time workers are employed in the public relations and advertising industries in occupations ranging from public relations specialist, public relations manager, and publicist; to copywriter, speechwriter, and editor; to art director, desktop publishing designer, and Webmaster; to research assistant, secretary, and office clerk.

Employment in public relations is expected to grow faster than the average for all industries through 2014, according to the U.S. Department of Labor. Competition for jobs will be strong, though, as the number of qualified applicants is expected to be much larger than the number of available positions. College graduates interested in public relations should narrow their interests to specific areas—such as community relations and crisis management—where public relations practitioners are needed. This will allow them to use specific skills and experience to distinguish themselves from the competition. Those with internship experience also will have the advantage when seeking permanent positions.

Competition among both foreign and domestic companies is fierce, forcing businesses to invest more money on promotion and public relations. A recent trend in public relations is damage control; for example the tobacco industry is fighting negative publicity with a focus on philanthropic efforts, the airline industry is spending significant budget dollars on encouraging people to fly after the terrorist attacks of September 11, 2001, and the auto and tire industries are trying to reassure customers that their products are safe after a number of fatal accidents were attributed to faulty tires.

Each article in *Careers in Focus: Public Relations* discusses a particular career in public relations in detail. The articles appear in Ferguson's *Encyclopedia of Careers and Vocational Guidance,* but have been updated and revised with the latest information from the U.S. Department of Labor, professional organizations, and other sources. In addition, the following new articles were created specifically for this book: Corporate Community Relations Directors, Public Relations Managers, and Publicists. The following paragraphs detail the sections and features that appear in the book.

The **Quick Facts** section provides a brief summary of the career, including recommended school subjects, personal skills, work environment, minimum educational requirements, salary ranges, certification or licensing requirements, and employment outlook. This section also provides acronyms and identification numbers for the following government classification indexes: the Dictionary of Occupational Titles (DOT), the Guide to Occupational Exploration (GOE), the National Occupational Classification (NOC) Index, and the Occupational Information Network (O*NET)-Standard Occupational Classification System (SOC) index. The DOT, GOE, and O*NET-SOC indexes have been created by the U.S. government; the NOC index is Canada's career classification system. Readers can use the identification numbers listed in the Quick Facts section to access further information about a career. Print editions of the DOT (O*NET Dictionary of Occupational Titles. Indianapolis, Ind.: JIST Works, 2004) and GOE (The Complete Guide for Occupational Exploration. Indianapolis, Ind.: JIST Works, 1993) are available at libraries. Electronic versions of the NOC (http://www23.hrdc-drhc. gc.ca) and O*NET-SOC (http://online.onetcenter.org) are available on the Internet. When no DOT, GOE, NOC, or O*NET-SOC numbers are present, this means that the U.S. Department of Labor or Human Resources Development Canada have not created a numerical designation for this career. In this instance, you will see the acronym "N/A," or not available.

The **Overview** section is a brief introductory description of the duties and responsibilities involved in this career. Oftentimes, a career may have a variety of job titles. When this is the case, alternative career titles are presented.

The **History** section describes the history of the particular job as it relates to the overall development of its industry or field.

The **Job** describes the primary and secondary duties of the job.

Requirements discusses high school and postsecondary education and training requirements, any certification or licensing that is necessary, and other personal requirements for success in the job.

Exploring offers suggestions on how to gain experience in or knowledge of the particular job before making a firm educational and financial commitment. The focus is on what can be done while still in high school (or in the early years of college) to gain a better understanding of the job.

The **Employers** section gives an overview of typical places of employment for the job.

Starting Out discusses the best ways to land that first job, be it through the college placement office, newspaper ads, or personal contact.

The **Advancement** section describes what kind of career path to expect from the job and how to get there.

Earnings lists salary ranges and describes the typical fringe benefits.

The **Work Environment** section describes the typical surroundings and conditions of employment—whether indoors or outdoors, noisy or quiet, social or independent. Also discussed are typical hours worked, any seasonal fluctuations, and the stresses and strains of the job.

The **Outlook** section summarizes the job in terms of the general economy and industry projections. For the most part, Outlook information is obtained from the U.S. Bureau of Labor Statistics and is supplemented by information taken from professional associations. Job growth terms follow those used in the *Occupational Outlook Handbook*. Growth described as "much faster than the average" means an increase of 27 percent or more. Growth described as "faster than the average" means an increase of 18 to 26 percent. Growth described as "about as fast as the average" means an increase of 9 to 17 percent. Growth described as "more slowly than the average" means an increase of 0 to 8 percent. "Decline" means a decrease by any amount.

Each article ends with **For More Information**, which lists organizations that provide information on training, education, internships, scholarships, and job placement.

Careers in Focus: Public Relations also includes photographs, informative sidebars, and interviews with professionals in the field.

Art Directors

OVERVIEW

Art directors play a key role in every stage of the creation of a public relations campaign, from formulating concepts to supervising production. Ultimately, they are responsible for planning and overseeing the presentation of their clients' messages in print or on screen—that is, in books, magazines, newspapers, television commercials, press releases, posters, and packaging, as well as in film and video and on the Internet.

In publishing, art directors work with artists, graphic designers, copywriters, photographers, and text editors to develop visual images and generate copy, according to the public relations strategy. They are responsible for evaluating existing illustrations, determining presentation styles and techniques, hiring both staff and freelance talent, working with layouts, and preparing budgets.

In films, videos, and television commercials, art directors set the general look of the visual elements and approve the props, costumes, and models. In addition, they are involved in casting, editing, and selecting the music.

There are approximately 10,000 art directors employed in the public relations and advertising industries in the United States.

QUICK FACTS

School Subjects
Art
Business
Computer science

Personal Skills
Artistic
Communication/ideas

Work Environment
Primarily indoors
Primarily one location

Minimum Education Level
Bachelor's degree

Salary Range
$36,610 to $63,950 to $125,890+

Certification or Licensing
None available

Outlook
Much faster than the average

DOT
164

GOE
01.02.03

NOC
5131

O*NET-SOC
27-1011.00

HISTORY

Artists have always been an important part of the creative process throughout history. In illustrating the first books, artists painted

Learn More About It

Cutlip, Scott M. *Effective Public Relations.* 9th ed. Upper Saddle River, N.J.: Prentice Hall, 2005.

Mogel, Leonard. *Making It in Public Relations: An Insider's Guide To Career Opportunities.* Mahwah, N.J.: Lawrence Erlbaum Associates, 2002.

Newsom, Doug, Judy Turk, and Dean Kruckeberg. *This is PR: The Realities of Public Relations.* Belmont, Calif.: Wadsworth Publishing, 2006.

Seitel, Fraser P. *The Practice of Public Relations.* 10th ed. Upper Saddle River, N.J.: Prentice Hall, 2006.

Stacks, Don W. *Primer of Public Relations Research.* New York: The Guilford Press, 2002.

Vault Editors. *Vault Guide to the Top Advertising & PR Employers.* New York: Vault Inc., 2007.

WetFeet. *Careers in Advertising and Public Relations.* San Francisco: WetFeet, 2006.

Wilcox, Dennis L. *Public Relations: Strategies and Tactics.* 8th ed. Boston: Allyn & Bacon, 2005.

their subjects by hand using a technique called illumination, which required putting egg-white tempera on vellum. Each copy of each book had to be printed and illustrated individually, often by the same person.

Printed illustrations first appeared in books in 1461. Through the years, prints were made through lithography, woodblock, and other means of duplicating images. Although making many copies of the same illustration was now possible, publishers still depended on individual artists to create the original works. Text editors usually decided what was to be illustrated and how, while artists commonly supervised the production of the artwork.

The first art directors were probably staff illustrators for book publishers. As the publishing industry grew more complex and incorporated new technologies such as photography and film, art direction evolved into a more supervisory position and became a full-time job.

Today's art directors supervise almost every type of visual project produced. Through a variety of methods and media, from television and film to magazines, press releases, and the Internet, art directors communicate ideas by selecting and supervising every element that goes into the finished product.

THE JOB

Art directors are responsible for all visual aspects of printed or on-screen projects. The art director oversees the process of developing visual solutions to a variety of communication problems. He or she helps to enhance books, magazines, newsletters, press releases, and other publications and creates television commercials, film and video productions, and Web sites. Some art directors with experience or knowledge in specific fields specialize in such areas as packaging, exhibitions and displays, or the Internet. But all directors, even those with specialized backgrounds, must be skilled in and knowledgeable about design, illustration, photography, computers, research, and writing in order to supervise the work of graphic artists, photographers, copywriters, text editors, and other employees.

Art directors may begin with the client's concept or develop one in collaboration with the copywriter and public relations specialist or manager. Once the goal is established (for example, a petroleum company's print campaign to educate customers about its green energy initiatives), the next step is to decide on the most effective way to communicate it. If there is text, for example, should the art director choose illustrations based on specific text references, or should the illustrations fill in the gaps in the copy? If a piece is being revised, existing illustrations must be reevaluated.

After deciding what needs to be illustrated, art directors must find sources that can create or provide the art. Photo agencies, for example, have photographs and illustrations on thousands of different subjects (in the case of the petroleum company's publicity campaign, perhaps images of healthy trees and plants, happy families at a picnic, etc.). If, however, the desired illustration does not exist, it may have to be commissioned or designed by one of the staff designers. Commissioning artwork means that the art director contacts a photographer or illustrator and explains what is needed. A price is negotiated, and the artist creates the image specifically for the art director.

Once the illustrations and other art elements have been secured, they must be presented in an appealing manner. The art director supervises (and may help in the production of) the layout of the piece and presents the final version to the client or creative director. Laying out is the process of figuring out where every image, headline, and block of text will be placed on the page. The size, style, and method of reproduction must all be specifically indicated so that the image is recreated as the director intended it.

In broadcast public relations and film and video, the art director has a wide variety of responsibilities and often interacts with an enormous number of creative professionals. Working with directors and producers, art directors interpret scripts and create or select settings in order to visually convey the story or the message. The art director oversees and channels the talents of set decorators and designers, model makers, location managers, propmasters, construction coordinators, and special effects people. In addition, art directors work with writers, unit production managers, cinematographers, costume designers, and postproduction staff, including editors and employees responsible for scoring and titles. The art director is ultimately responsible for all visual aspects of the finished product.

The process of producing a PR-oriented television commercial (for example, a commercial that details a major corporation's scholarship program) begins in much the same way that a printed public relations piece is created. The art director may start with the client's concept or create one in-house in collaboration with staff members. Once a concept has been created and the copywriter has generated the corresponding text, the art director sketches a rough storyboard based on the writer's ideas, and the plan is presented for review to the creative director. The next step is to develop a finished storyboard, with larger and more detailed frames (the individual scenes) in color. This storyboard is presented to the client for review and used as a guide for the film director as well.

Technology is playing an increasingly important role in the art director's job. Most art directors, for example, use a variety of computer software programs, including Adobe InDesign, FrameMaker, Illustrator, and Photoshop; QuarkXPress; and CorelDRAW. Many others create and oversee Web sites for clients and work with other interactive media and materials, including CD-ROM, touch screens, multidimensional visuals, and new animation programs.

Art directors usually work on more than one project at a time and must be able to keep numerous, unrelated details straight. They often work under pressure of a deadline and yet must remain calm and pleasant when dealing with clients and staff. Because they are supervisors, art directors are often called upon to resolve problems, not only with projects but with employees as well.

Art directors are not entry-level workers. They usually have years of experience working at lower-level jobs in the field before gaining the knowledge needed to supervise projects. Depending on whether they work primarily in publishing or film, art directors have to know how printing presses operate or how film is processed. They should also be familiar with a variety of production techniques in order to understand the wide range of ways that images can be manipulated to meet the needs of a project.

REQUIREMENTS

High School

A variety of high school courses will give you both a taste of college-level offerings and an idea of the skills necessary for art directors on-the-job. These courses include art, drawing, art history, graphic design, illustration, photography, public relations, advertising, and desktop publishing.

Math courses are also important. Most of the elements of sizing an image involve calculating percentage reduction or enlargement of the original picture. This must be done with a great degree of accuracy if the overall design is going to work. For example, type size may have to be figured within a thirty-second of an inch for a print project. Errors can be extremely costly and may make the project look sloppy.

Other useful courses that you should take in high school include business, computing, English, technical drawing, cultural studies, psychology, and social science.

Postsecondary Training

A college degree is usually a requirement for art directors; however, in some instances, it is not absolutely necessary. According to the American Institute of Graphic Arts, nine out of 10 artists have a college degree. Among them, six out of 10 have majored in graphic design, and two out of 10 have majored in fine arts. In addition, almost two out of 10 have a master's degree. Along with general two- and four-year colleges and universities, a number of professional art schools offer two-, three-, or four-year programs with such classes as figure drawing, painting, graphic design, and other art courses, as well as classes in art history, writing, business administration, communications, and foreign languages.

Courses in public relations, advertising, marketing, photography, filmmaking, set direction, layout, desktop publishing, and fashion are also important for those interested in becoming art directors. Specialized courses, sometimes offered only at professional art schools, may be particularly helpful for students who want to go into art direction. These include typography, animation, storyboard, Web site design, and portfolio development.

Because of the rapidly increasing use of computers in design work, it is essential to have a thorough understanding of how computer art and layout programs work. In smaller companies, the art director may be responsible for operating this equipment; in larger companies, a staff person, under the direction of the art director, may use these programs. In either case, the director must know what can be done with the available equipment.

In addition to course work at the college level, many universities and professional art schools offer graduates or students in their final year a variety of workshop projects, desktop publishing training opportunities, and internships. These programs provide students with opportunities to develop their personal design styles as well as their portfolios.

Other Requirements

The work of an art director requires creativity, imagination, curiosity, and a sense of adventure. Art directors must be able to work with all sorts of specialized equipment and computer software, such as graphic design programs, as well as make presentations on the ideas behind their work.

The ability to work well with different people and organizations is a must for art directors. They must always be up-to-date on new techniques, trends, and attitudes. And because deadlines are a constant part of the work, an ability to handle stress and pressure well is key.

Accuracy and attention to detail are important parts of the job. When art is done neatly and correctly, the public usually pays no notice. But when a project is done poorly or sloppily, people will notice, even if they have had no design training. Other requirements for art directors include time management skills and an interest in media and people's motivations and lifestyles.

EXPLORING

High school students can get an idea of what an art director does by working on the staff of the school newspaper, magazine, or yearbook. It may also be possible to secure a part-time job assisting the community relations director of the local newspaper or to work at a public relations firm. Developing your own artistic talent is important, and this can be accomplished through self-training (reading books and practicing) or through courses in painting, drawing, or other creative arts. At the very least, you should develop your "creative eye," that is, your ability to develop ideas visually. One way to do this is by familiarizing yourself with great works, such as paintings or highly creative magazine ads, motion pictures, videos, or commercials.

Students can also become members of a variety of art clubs around the nation. If you have access to the Internet, check out Paleta: The Art Project (http://www.paletaworld.org) to join a free art club. In addition to keeping members up-to-date on industry trends, such clubs offer job information, resources, and a variety of other benefits.

EMPLOYERS

Approximately 10,000 art directors are employed in the public relations and advertising industries in the United States. They also work at advertising agencies, publishing houses, museums, packaging firms, photography studios, marketing firms, desktop publishing outfits, digital prepress houses, or printing companies. Art directors who oversee and produce onscreen products often work for film production houses, Web designers, multimedia developers, computer games developers, or television stations.

While companies of all sizes employ art directors, smaller organizations often combine the positions of graphic designer, illustrator, and art director. And although opportunities for art direction can be found all across the nation and abroad, many larger firms in such cities as Chicago, New York, and Los Angeles usually have more openings, as well as higher pay scales, than smaller companies.

STARTING OUT

Since an art director's job requires a great deal of experience, it is usually not considered an entry-level position. Typically, a person on a career track toward art director is hired as an assistant to an established director. Recent graduates wishing to enter public relations should have a portfolio of their work containing seven to 10 samples to demonstrate their understanding of both the business and the media in which they want to work.

Serving as an intern is a good way to get experience and develop skills. Graduates should also consider taking an entry-level job in a publisher's art department to gain initial experience. Either way, aspiring art directors must be willing to acquire their credentials by working on various projects. This may mean working in a variety of areas, such as public relations, advertising, marketing, editing, and design.

College publications offer students a chance to gain experience and develop portfolios. In addition, many students are able to do freelance work while still in school, allowing them to make important industry contacts and gain on-the-job experience at the same time.

ADVANCEMENT

While some may be content upon reaching the position of art director to remain there, many art directors take on even more responsibility within their organizations, become television directors, start their own public relations agencies, create their own Web sites, develop original multimedia programs, or launch their own magazines.

Many people who get to the position of art director do not advance beyond the title but move on to work at more prestigious firms. Competition for positions at companies that have national reputations continues to be keen because of the sheer number of talented people interested. At smaller publications or local companies, the competition may be less intense, since candidates are competing primarily against others in the local market.

EARNINGS

The job title of art director can mean many different things, depending on the company at which the director is employed. According to the U.S. Department of Labor, beginning art directors or an art director who worked at a small firm earned $36,610 or less per year in 2005; experienced art directors working at larger companies earned more than $125,890. The median annual earnings for art directors were $63,950. (Again, it is important to note that these positions are not entry level; beginning art directors have probably already accumulated several years of experience in the field for which they were paid far less.)

According to the American Institute of Graphic Arts' Aquent Salary Survey 2003, the median salary for art directors was $60,000. Art directors in the 25th percentile earned $48,000 annually, while those in the 75th percentile made $75,000 per year.

Most companies employing art directors offer insurance benefits, a retirement plan, and other incentives and bonuses.

WORK ENVIRONMENT

Art directors usually work in studios or office buildings. While their work areas are ordinarily comfortable, well lit, and ventilated, they often handle glue, paint, ink, and other materials that pose safety hazards, and they should, therefore, exercise caution.

Art directors at art and design studios and publishing and public relations firms usually work a standard 40-hour week. Many, however, work overtime during busy periods in order to meet deadlines. Similarly, directors at film and video operations and at television studios work as many hours as required—usually many more than 40 per week—in order to finish projects according to predetermined schedules.

While art directors work independently while reviewing artwork and reading copy, much of their time is spent collaborating with and supervising a team of employees, often consisting of copywriters, editors, photographers, graphic artists, and public relations specialists.

OUTLOOK

The extent to which art director positions are in demand, like many other positions, depends on the economy in general; when times are tough, people and businesses spend less, and cutbacks are made. When the economy is healthy, employment prospects for art directors will be favorable. The U.S. Department of Labor predicts that employment for art directors in public relations and advertising will grow much faster than the average for all occupations through 2014. However, it is important to note that the supply of aspiring artists is expected to exceed the number of job openings. As a result, those wishing to enter the field will encounter keen competition for salaried, staff positions as well as for freelance work. And although the Internet is expected to provide many opportunities for artists and art directors, some firms are hiring employees without formal art or design training to operate computer-aided design systems and oversee work.

FOR MORE INFORMATION

For more information on design professionals, contact
American Institute of Graphic Arts
164 Fifth Avenue
New York, NY 10010-5901
Tel: 212-807-1990
http://www.aiga.org

The Art Directors Club is an international, nonprofit organization of directors in public relations, advertising, graphic design, interactive media, broadcast design, typography, packaging, environmental design, photography, illustration, and related disciplines. For information, contact
The Art Directors Club
106 West 29th Street
New York, NY 10001-5301
Tel: 212-643-1440
Email: info@adcglobal.org
http://www.adcglobal.org

For information on the graphic arts, contact
Graphic Artists Guild
32 Broadway, Suite 1114
New York, NY 10004-1612
Tel: 212-791-3400
http://www.gag.org

For information on student membership, contact
Public Relations Society of America
33 Maiden Lane, 11th Floor
New York, NY 10038-5150
Tel: 212-460-1400
Email: prssa@prsa.org (student membership)
http://www.prsa.org

Copywriters

OVERVIEW

Copywriters express, promote, and interpret ideas and facts in written form for books, magazines, trade journals, newspapers, technical studies and reports, company newsletters, press releases, radio and television broadcasts, and advertisements.

Most copywriters are employed in the advertising industry. Their main goal is to persuade the general public to choose or favor certain goods, services, and personalities. Copywriters also may work for public relations firms or in communications departments of large companies.

HISTORY

Copywriters have been in demand by public relations firms as long as there has been a need to effectively communicate ideas and news to the general public, as well as to government agencies, corporations, and other organizations that might purchase a company's products or use its services.

THE JOB

Many corporations, nonprofit groups, and governmental agencies employ copywriters within their public relations departments to promote their businesses or philanthropic and cultural projects. Copywriters produce a variety of materials ranging from brochures, newsletters, annual reports, press releases, Web site content, speeches, and other promotional materials.

For example, copywriters employed at Abbott Laboratories, a global health care company, might be enlisted to help promote a philanthropic project such as a recent yearlong health and human service drive in Illinois. Copywriters would need to research the scope of the event—details of the types of services available, amount of money raised and disbursed, the contributors and beneficiaries of the project, and other information. They would then promote the event with write-ups in company newsletters and at its Web site, in brochures and industry magazines, and in press releases to local media outlets. Copywriters must be able to write in different voices; they need to identify the main audience of a press release or promotional material and use the appropriate tone and jargon in order to hold the reader's attention.

A copywriter's main duty, however, is to promote the company's industry presence. Copywriters employed at the Red Cross, a worldwide charitable organization, might be assigned to write articles regarding current social service programs, disaster relief projects, or holiday fund-raising campaigns. Copywriters often work with members of the marketing department to create promotional products such as brochures and media kits, as well as content for the organization's Web site. They may at times consult with photographers and graphic designers in order to create material that is both informational and visually pleasing. Other tasks may include maintaining a database of contributors, photo files, creating multimedia presentations, and responding to requests for more company information.

Public relations copywriters are usually salaried workers, though freelance work is also available in this field. Freelance copywriters are often employed by smaller companies whose size does not warrant a full-time copywriter or by a new business. Freelance copywriters have the same duties as those employed full time, such as creating promotional pieces, press releases, and information for Web sites. However, in dealing with multiple clients with a variety of business interests and goals, freelancers need to be quick learners, versatile, and capable of working on multiple projects simultaneously. They also must provide their own office space and equipment such as computers and fax machines. Freelancers also are responsible for keeping tax records, sending out invoices, negotiating contracts, and providing their own health insurance.

REQUIREMENTS
High School
While in high school, build a broad educational foundation by taking courses in English, literature, foreign languages, business, computer science, and typing. You should be confident in your typing abilities and comfortable with computer programs,

as copywriters use computers everyday for writing, researching, and development.

Postsecondary Training

Competition for writing jobs almost always demands the background of a college education. Many employers prefer that you have a broad liberal arts background or majors in English, literature, history, philosophy, or one of the social sciences. Other employers desire communications, journalism, or public relations training in college. A number of schools offer courses in copywriting and other business writing.

In addition to formal course work, most employers look for practical writing experience. If you have served on high school or college newspapers, yearbooks, or literary magazines, you will make a better candidate, as well as if you have worked for small community newspapers or radio stations, even in an unpaid position. Many public relations firms offer summer internship programs that can provide valuable writing experience. Interns do many simple tasks, such as running errands and answering phones, but some may be asked to perform research and even assist with the writing.

Other Requirements

To be a copywriter, you should be creative and able to express ideas clearly, have a broad general knowledge, be a skilled researcher, and be computer literate. Other assets include curiosity, persistence, initiative, resourcefulness, and an accurate memory. At some public relations firms and other employers, the environment is hectic and client deadlines are short. For these copywriters, the ability to concentrate and produce under pressure is essential.

EXPLORING

As a high school or college student, you can test your interest and aptitude in the field of writing by serving as a reporter or writer on school newspapers, yearbooks, and literary magazines. Various writing courses and workshops will offer you the opportunity to sharpen your writing skills.

Small community newspapers and local radio stations often welcome contributions from outside sources, although they may not have the resources to pay for them. Jobs in bookstores, magazine shops, and even newsstands will offer you a chance to become familiar with various publications.

You can also obtain information on writing as a career by visiting public relations firms, local newspapers, publishers, or radio and television stations and interviewing some of the writers who work there. Career conferences and other guidance programs frequently include speakers on the entire field of communications from local or national organizations.

EMPLOYERS

There are more than 7,800 public relations firms nationwide. Copywriters and editors hold approximately 8,000 jobs in the industry.

STARTING OUT

Most copywriters start out in entry-level positions, working as office assistants or copywriting assistants. These jobs may be listed with college career services offices or in the want ads of local papers. You can also try applying directly to the hiring departments of public relations firms or other large companies that have public relations departments. Graduates who previously served internships with these companies often have the advantage of knowing someone who can give them a personal recommendation.

Employers will often ask to see samples of published writing. These samples should be assembled in an organized portfolio or scrapbook. Bylined or signed articles are more credible (and, as a result, more useful) than stories whose source is not identified.

Beginning positions as a copywriting assistant usually involve library research, preparation of rough ad drafts, and other related writing tasks. These are generally carried on under the supervision of a senior copywriter.

ADVANCEMENT

Advancement may be more rapid in small public relations agencies or companies, where beginners learn by doing a little bit of everything and may be given writing tasks immediately. In large firms, duties are usually more compartmentalized. Assistants in entry-level positions are assigned such tasks as research, fact checking, and copyrighting, but it generally takes much longer to advance to full-scale copywriting duties.

Promotion as a copywriter usually takes the form of obtaining more projects for larger and more influential clients. For example, being assigned to work on press releases for a large corporation would be viewed as an impressive achievement. Others advance by moving to a larger or more prestigious firm or starting up their own business.

Freelance or self-employed writers earn advancement in the form of larger fees as they gain exposure and establish their reputations.

EARNINGS

According to the U.S. Department of Labor (USDL), median annual salaries for writers in advertising and related services was $57,400 in 2005. In 2005, median annual earnings for salaried writers (including copywriters) were $46,420 a year, according to the USDL. The lowest paid 10 percent earned less than $24,320, while the highest paid 10 percent earned $89,940 or more.

In addition to their salaries, many writers earn some income from freelance work. Part-time freelancers may earn from $5,000 to $15,000 a year. Freelance earnings vary widely. Full-time established freelance writers may earn more than $75,000 a year.

WORK ENVIRONMENT

Working conditions vary for copywriters, depending on the size of their employer and whether or not they frequently work under tight deadlines. Though their workweek usually runs 35 to 40 hours, many copywriters work overtime, working nights and weekends to meet client deadlines.

Though copywriters do some of their work independently, they often must cooperate with artists, photographers, editors, and other public relations professionals who may have widely differing ideas of how the materials should be prepared and presented.

Physical surroundings range from comfortable private offices to noisy, crowded offices filled with other workers typing and talking on the telephone. Some copywriters must confine their research to the library or telephone interviews, but others may travel to other cities or countries or to client work sites.

The work is arduous, but most copywriters are seldom bored. The most difficult element is the continual pressure of deadlines. People who are the most content as copywriters enjoy and work well with deadline pressure.

OUTLOOK

Employment for writers and authors in the public relations industry is projected to grow by 20 percent through 2014, according to the U.S. Department of Labor. Smaller agencies and home-based businesses are on the rise; however, the mega-agencies—multinational agencies created from mergers and acquisitions—still dominate the industry. Of the more than 7,800 public relations agencies in the United States, most of the large firms are located in New York, Chicago, and Los Angeles and offer higher pay scales than smaller agencies.

People entering this field should realize that the competition for jobs is extremely keen. The appeal of public relations jobs will continue to grow, as many young graduates find the industry glamorous and exciting.

FOR MORE INFORMATION

For information on accreditation, contact
International Association of Business Communicators
One Hallidie Plaza, Suite 600
San Francisco, CA 94102-2818
Tel: 415-544-4700
http://www.iabc.com

For statistics, salary surveys, and information on accreditation and student membership, contact
Public Relations Society of America
33 Maiden Lane, 11th Floor
New York, NY 10038-5150
Tel: 212-460-1400
Email: prssa@prsa.org (student membership)
http://www.prsa.org

INTERVIEW

Dr. Terry Rentner is an associate professor and chair of the Department of Journalism at Bowling Green State University (BGSU) in Bowling Green, Ohio. She has taught all levels of public relations courses, including the senior-level capstone course, Public Relations Campaigns. She was public relations sequence head for 16 years before becoming department chair. This is her 19th year advising the BGSU chapter of the Public Relations Student Society of America. She also has written several book chapters on integrating service learning in the public relations curriculum.

Dr. Rentner's research focuses on high-risk drinking reduction among college students. It is grounded in theory (social norms) and has led to the development of social norms programs implemented in college and universities across the nation. In 2000, her alcohol research program was named one of the top seven model programs in the nation by the U.S. Department of Education. Dr. Rentner discussed the education of public relations students with the editors of Careers in Focus: Public Relations.

Q. Can you tell us about the public relations program at Bowling Green State University (BGSU)?

A. The public relations sequence is one of three sequences in the Department of Journalism at BGSU. The other two sequences are print and broadcast. Our public relations (PR) sequence offers classes detailing the principles and writing involved in public relations, as well as media publication and design, and a capstone campaigns course. In addition, PR students must take Introduction to Mass Communication, Introduction to Journalistic Writing, Reporting, Law and Ethics, and complete two internships. Students also chose at least one issues course in mass communication and a skills course from another sequence. Students are also required to take marketing and management courses. Public relations students are prepared for careers in the field such as corporate, nonprofit, agency, health, and government public relations. The Department of Journalism is accredited through the Accrediting Council in Journalism and Mass Communication, one of only 109 programs in the country.

Q. What are the most important personal and professional qualities for public relations majors?

A. These include:

- Strong writing skills.
- Management skills.
- Ability to multitask.
- Ability to work in groups.
- Ability to work with people from various ethnic backgrounds who have different cultural experiences than their own.
- Strong organizational skills.
- Ability to write for various media and publics.
- Ability to create simple promotional pieces and consult with design experts on more difficult ones.
- Good presentation skills.
- Good reporting skills.
- Excellent understanding of law and public relations ethics.
- Membership in the Public Relations Student Society of America while in college, and the Public Relations Society of America (PRSA) as a professional.

Q. What advice would you offer public relations majors as they graduate and look for jobs?

A. • Focus on your internship experiences while in school.
   • Prepare a portfolio for interviews.
   • Have a faculty member or expert review your resume and cover letter.
   • Do not send out generic resumes and cover letters; tailor them to a specific position announcement or inquire about an informational interview with the organization.
   • Dress professionally.
   • Keep in touch with your professors—one of the best ways to hear of entry-level jobs.
   • Join the PRSA as soon as you graduate.
   • Keep in touch with organizations where you interned; they may not have positions now, but possibly in the future, and they may likely know of other positions.

Q. Can you tell us about the internship opportunities that are available to students at your school?

A. Our students must complete two internships—one on campus and one off campus.

On-campus opportunities (not inclusive of all opportunities):
   • Office of Marketing and Communications
   • Athletic office
   • Bowen-Thompson Student Union Event Planning
   • College of Musical Arts
   • College of Education
   • BG News (daily paper)
   • BG 24-News (television station)
   • Key yearbook
   • Student Health Services
   • Dance marathon

Off-campus opportunities (not inclusive of all opportunities):
   • Agency public relations at both small and large firms throughout the United States
   • Disney World and other entertainment entities throughout the country
   • Hospitals and health care facilities
   • Nonprofit organizations such as the American Red Cross, Big Brothers/Big Sisters, etc.
   • Corporate public relations
   • Athletic organizations
   • Educational institutions

Corporate Community Relations Directors

OVERVIEW

Corporate community relations directors work to promote a positive image of corporations through various forms of philanthropy, such as educational programs, grants, and cultural and sporting events. They are responsible for researching, planning, implementing, and advertising these outreach programs. Oftentimes, corporate community relations directors act as liaisons between the corporation and community, nonprofit groups, local government, and the media.

HISTORY

The first documented public relations firm was established in the early 1900s. Run by newspaper veterans, the Publicity Bureau had Harvard University as its first client.

Many corporations, regardless of their industry-focus or size, realize the importance of positive publicity. One well-placed news item can be considered priceless in terms of advertising and name recognition. Also, the notion of global citizenship has had a huge impact on the growth of corporate public relations. It is not enough for companies to succeed in a particular arena. As a global citizen, a company must react and help address social and health issues, environmental concerns, education reform, and cultural advancement. For this reason, corporations have seen the need to establish public relations departments to develop, implement, and report on such programs.

Undergraduate public relations students discuss a lecture point with their professor after class. *(The Image Works)*

The Public Relations Society of America is the world's largest professional organization catering to this industry. It has more than 28,000 members, many of whom specialize in corporate public relations.

THE JOB

Corporations, both large and small, have recognized the benefits of maintaining a positive image with their employees, shareholders and competing businesses. Many corporations today also work hard to uphold this image with the public as well. Corporate community relations directors are responsible for developing and implementing strategies to establish good relations between their employer and the community. They act as a company liaison to the community, other businesses, the government, the media, and various interest groups.

Some corporate community relations departments have programs that promote a particular business product or service. The computer giant IBM, for example, has taken an interest in boosting the computer science skills of high schools students by providing free access to computer science resources. Other companies may task their corporate community relations team to implement programs or sponsor events unrelated to their main business practice. For example, LaSalle Bank, part of a major worldwide banking conglomerate, has long been a major sponsor of many sporting and family oriented events in the Chicago area, such as the Chicago Marathon, the Shamrock Shuffle, the Winter WonderFest, and various concerts. While these events enrich the lives of many Chicagoans, especially in the areas of sports and culture, they also provide priceless promotion, name recognition, and positive public relations for the corporation.

Corporate community relations directors also recognize the benefits of working within the local community the company serves. Directors employed by Target Corporation, for example, help improve local schools, libraries, and neighborhood music programs by developing programs that provide assistance through financial or product donations and matching grants.

Corporate community relations directors use a variety of methods to demonstrate their company's corporate citizenship. They may encourage employee participation in community events such as blood and clothing drives, charitable giving at holiday specific events (such as Toys for Tots), and financial donations during times of national crisis. They may recruit employees to volunteer at food pantries or participate as tutors or mentors to inner city children. Corporate community relations directors may also assemble employee teams to represent the company at sporting events, whether as competitors or volunteers.

The ability to communicate well is imperative in this career. Corporate community relations directors work closely with all forms of media—newspapers and magazines, television, radio, and the Internet—often providing press releases that detail their company's latest philanthropic projects. They are often responsible for posting summaries of these activities at their company's Web site. The Chief Executive Officer or another company executive may consult with the corporate community relations team before meeting with shareholders or attending a public event. Directors may be asked to help write speeches, or give a speech when acting as the company's representative. At times they might need to use their media savvy to troubleshoot any conflicts between the company and the community. A good corporate community relations director is able to "spin" any crisis situation to portray their company in the best light possible.

Experienced corporate community relations directors may conduct public tours of the company facilities. They may also be in charge of organizing the opening of a corporate-sponsored art show, awards dinner, or traveling museum exhibit. They may need to contact event planners to organize catering and setup services, hire photographers to document the event, and work with designers to provide input on the design of invitations for the gala, among other tasks.

REQUIREMENTS

High School

Take English and creative writing courses to strengthen your writing talents. Also, you can begin to hone your public speaking skills by taking classes in communication and speech, or you can even join your high school debate team. Does your high school offer classes or clubs in mass media? Outlets such as your campus radio or cable television station, or even the school newspaper, can offer a wealth of experience in dealing with the press.

Postsecondary Training

A minimum of a four-year degree is the norm in this field, with majors in public relations, communications, marketing, or journalism the typical educational path. It is possible to enter public relations with other degrees—for example, a liberal arts degree—but taking some coursework in public relations or communications will certainly be useful.

Some colleges, such as George Mason University, also offer undergraduate concentrations in corporate community relations and related subjects. Advanced coursework in corporate public relations is also available at some colleges and universities.

Certification or Licensing

There is no specific certification available for corporate community relations directors, but the Public Relations Society of America and the International Association of Business Communicators accredit public relations workers who have at least five years of experience in the field and pass a comprehensive examination. Such accreditation is a sign of competence in this field, although it is not a requirement for employment.

Other Requirements

Being a people person is one of the most important qualifications for this job. As a corporate community relations director, you will need to interact effectively with company executives, colleagues, civic leaders, representatives from various charities and educational and cultural groups, and the public. The public relations department often works as a team in order to complete a project, exhibit, or charity event. It is also important to be a quick thinker, organized, and outgoing—almost to the point of being aggressive. This might not be the right career for those who are shy.

The ability to communicate well is key. You will frequently be asked to write speeches, press releases, or brochures documenting your company's latest philanthropic project. Your verbal skills will also be tested when giving presentations, interviews, or presiding over a press conference.

A love of volunteering and commitment to others are other helpful traits to have in this career.

EXPLORING

You can act as a public relations specialist for your school, scout troop, or sports team. Organize a book and toy drive to benefit kids at a local shelter, send a box of supplies to troops stationed overseas, or simply organize your friends to clean up litter in the park. Afterward, you can send a press release documenting your good deeds, the participants, and any other details to your local newspaper, cable network, or radio station. Your group will not only gain name recognition, but satisfaction in giving back to the community.

EMPLOYERS

Employment opportunities exist with large or middle-size corporations whose needs warrant a public relations department. Many major corporations are located in large cities such as New York, Los Angeles, Dallas, Denver, Seattle, Atlanta, and Chicago, but opportunities are available throughout the United States. Prospective employers come from a variety of industries—from computer manufacturers to retail conglomerates to banking giants.

Freelance work can be found with smaller companies that may contract public relations specialists on a project-to-project basis.

STARTING OUT

Entry-level work is usually found as an assistant within public relations departments at corporations and other organizations. As an assistant you may be asked to help with travel arrangements, organize awards for a corporate-sponsored sporting event, send out company holiday greeting cards, or prepare media kits and Microsoft PowerPoint presentations.

ADVANCEMENT

With experience, you may be promoted to head of the public relations or community relations department. Aside from overseeing the performance of the staff, the director may be asked to serve as official spokesperson for the corporation, or serve as a board member of a community group.

Moving to a larger corporation, perhaps one that deals with more numerous and larger scale philanthropic projects, is another form of job advancement.

Other corporate community relations directors leave the corporate world to teach at the secondary and postsecondary levels.

EARNINGS

The U.S. Department of Labor does not provide salary information for corporate community relations directors, but it does provide data for public relations managers and public relations specialists. In 2005, salaries for public relations managers ranged from less than $40,870 to more than $106,440, with a median of $76,450. Public relations specialists earned salaries that ranged from $26,870 to more than $84,300, with a median of $45,020.

Benefit and compensation packages for corporate community relations directors are usually excellent, and may even include such things as bonuses, stock awards, and company-paid insurance premiums.

WORK ENVIRONMENT

Corporate community relations directors work in comfortable, well-lit offices. They spend much of their day on the telephone, conducting interviews, organizing volunteers, and calling vendors. They also use computers to write news releases and send them to various media outlets, track expenses and staff hours, and send e-mail to coworkers, the media, and the public. The atmosphere may be frenzied at times, especially when the department is working on multiple projects. Most corporate community relations directors work a normal 40-hour week. However, they often work evenings and weekends when most projects such as mentoring programs, sporting events, or community galas take place.

OUTLOOK

Strong community relations and outreach play a key role in the success of businesses today. In the wake of corporate scandals, consumers are holding corporations to higher standards in exchange for their customer loyalty. As a result, corporate community relations directors will be in strong demand as corporations seek to educate the media, government agencies, and the public about the actions of their companies and their community outreach programs.

FOR MORE INFORMATION

For information on accreditation, contact
International Association of Business Communicators
One Hallidie Plaza, Suite 600
San Francisco, CA 94102-2818
Tel: 415-544-4700
http://www.iabc.com

For statistics, salary surveys, and information on accreditation and student membership, contact
Public Relations Society of America
33 Maiden Lane, 11th Floor
New York, NY 10038-5150
Tel: 212-460-1400
Email: prssa@prsa.org (student membership)
http://www.prsa.org

Demographers

OVERVIEW

Demographers are population specialists who collect and analyze vital statistics related to human population changes, such as births, marriages, and deaths. They plan and conduct research surveys to study population trends and assess the effects of population movements. Demographers work for government organizations as well as at private companies across the country.

HISTORY

Population studies of one kind or another have always been of interest for various reasons. As early as the mid-1600s, for example, the English were the first to systematically record and register all births and deaths. Over the years, recording techniques were refined and expanded to conduct more sophisticated population surveys so that governments could collect information, such as number of people and extent of property holdings, to measure wealth and levy taxes.

In recent years, census taking has become much more comprehensive, and the scientific methods of collecting and interpreting demographic information have also improved extensively. Demographers now have a leading role in developing detailed population studies that are designed to reveal the essential characteristics of a society, such as the availability of health care or average income levels.

QUICK FACTS

School Subjects
Computer science
Mathematics
Sociology

Personal Skills
Communication/ideas
Technical/scientific

Work Environment
Primarily indoors
One location with some travel

Minimum Education Level
Bachelor's degree

Salary Range
$36,590 to $62,650 to $99,500+

Certification or Licensing
None available

Outlook
More slowly than the average

DOT
054

GOE
02.04.02

NOC
2161

O*NET-SOC
15-2041.00, 19-3099.00

THE JOB

Demography is a social science that organizes population facts into a statistical analysis. A demographer works to establish ways in

Other Opportunities in Public Relations

The public relations industry offers a variety of career paths to people from all educational backgrounds. Here are just a few of the additional options not covered in this book:

- Accountants and auditors
- Intellectual property lawyers
- Computer software engineers
- Multimedia artists and animators
- Editors
- Business managers
- Computer programmers
- Computer and Internet security specialists
- Webmasters
- Web developers
- Customer service representatives
- Office clerks
- Bookkeeping, accounting, and auditing clerks
- Security workers
- Data entry and information processing workers
- Mail clerks and mail machine operators

which numbers may be organized to produce new and useful information. For example, demographers may study data collected on the frequency of disease in a certain area, develop graphs and charts to plot the spread of that disease, and then forecast the probability that the medical problem may spread.

Many demographers work on the basis of a sampling technique in which the characteristics of the whole population are judged by taking a sample of a part of it. For example, demographers may collect data on the educational level of residents living in various locations throughout a community. They can use this information to make a projection of the average educational level of the community as a whole. In this way, demographers conduct research and forecast trends on various social and economic patterns throughout an area.

Demographers not only conduct their own surveys but often work with statistics gathered from government sources, private surveys, and public opinion polls. They may compare different statistical information, such as an area's average income level and its population, and use it to forecast the community's future educational and medical needs. They may tabulate the average age, income, educational levels, crime rate, and poverty rate of a farming community and compare the results with the same statistics of an urban environment.

Computers have radically changed the role of the demographer. Now, much greater amounts of data can be collected and analyzed. In the Bureau of Census, for example, demographers work with material that has been compiled from the nationwide census conducted every 10 years. Millions of pieces of demographic information, such as age, gender, occupation, educational level, and country of origin, are collected from people around the country. A demographer may take this statistical information, analyze it, and then use it to forecast population growth or economic trends.

Demographers investigate and analyze a variety of social science questions for the government, such as rates of illness, availability of health and police services, and other issues that define a community. Private companies may use the information to make marketing decisions, such as where to open a new store and how best to reach possible customers.

Demographers may work on long-range planning. Population trends are especially important in such areas as educational and economic planning, and a demographer's analysis is often used to help set policy on health care issues and a host of other social concerns. Local, state, and national government agencies all use the demographer's statistical forecasts in an attempt to accurately provide transportation, education, and other services.

Demographers may teach demographic research techniques to students. They also work as consultants to private businesses. Much of their time is spent doing library research, analyzing demographic information of various population groups.

An *applied statistician,* a specialized type of demographer, uses accepted theories and known statistical formulas to collect and analyze data in a specific area, such as the availability of health care in a specified location.

REQUIREMENTS

High School

Since you will need at least a bachelor's degree to find work as a demographer, you should take college preparatory courses, such as social studies, English, and mathematics (algebra and geometry) while in high school. In addition, take any statistics classes that your school offers. Training in computer science is also advantageous, as computers are used extensively for research and statistical analysis.

Postsecondary Training

College course work should include classes in social research methods, public policy, public health, statistics, and computer applications. Keep in mind that while you can get some starting jobs in the field with a bachelor's degree, most social scientists go on to attain advanced degrees. Many demographers get a doctorate in statistics, sociology, or demography. Approximately 110 universities offer master's programs in statistics, and about 60 have statistics departments offering doctorate programs.

Other Requirements

To work as a demographer, you should enjoy using logic to solve problems and have an aptitude for mathematics. You should also enjoy detailed work and must like to study and learn. Research experience is helpful. Other qualities that are helpful include intellectual curiosity and creativity, good written and oral communication skills, objectivity, and systematic work habits.

EXPLORING

A part-time or summer job at a company with a statistical research department is a good way of gaining insight into the career of demographer. Discussions with professional demographers are another way of learning about the rewards and responsibilities in this field. While in high school, ask your mathematics teachers to give you some simple statistical problems related to population changes in order to practice the kinds of statistical techniques that demographers use. Exploring statistical surveys and information from The Gallup Organization on the Internet (http://www.gallup.com) is another way to learn about this career. Additionally, undertaking your own demographic survey of an organization or group, such as your school or after-school club, is a project worth considering.

EMPLOYERS

Federal agencies such as the Census Bureau and the Bureau of Labor Statistics employ a large number of demographers, as do local and state government agencies. Private industry (including large public relations firms) also may use the services of demographers, as well as universities, colleges, and foundations. Some demographers work as independent consultants rather than full-time employees for any one organization.

STARTING OUT

The usual method of entering the profession is through completion of an undergraduate or graduate degree in sociology or public health with an emphasis in demographic methods. According to Cary Davis, former vice president of the Population Reference Bureau in Washington, D.C., however, most entry-level positions require a graduate degree. "In fact," says Davis, "no one on my staff knows of any demographer who has less than a master's degree. Focus on an area that interests you, such as births and deaths or public health."

Qualified applicants can apply directly to private research firms or other companies that do population studies. University career services offices can help identify such organizations. Government jobs are listed with the Office of Personnel Management.

ADVANCEMENT

According to Cary Davis, demographers who narrow their focus and become specialized in an area of interest are most likely to advance. Those with the highest degree of education are also most likely to be promoted.

EARNINGS

Earnings vary widely according to education, training, and place of employment. Social scientists earned a median annual salary of approximately $62,650 in 2005, according to the U.S. Department of Labor. Salaries ranged from less than $36,590 to more than $99,500. In 2005, statisticians (often including demographers) had median annual earnings of $62,450. Vacation days and other benefits, such as sick leave, group insurance, and a retirement plan, are typically offered to demographers working full time for any large organization.

WORK ENVIRONMENT

Most demographers work in offices or classrooms during a regular 40-hour week. Depending on the project and deadlines, however, overtime may be required. Those engaged in research may work with other demographers assembling related information. Most of the work revolves around analyzing population data or interpreting computer information. A demographer is also usually responsible for writing a report detailing the findings. Some travel may be required, such as to attend a conference or complete limited field research.

OUTLOOK

According to the U.S. Department of Labor, the social science field is expected to grow more slowly than the average through 2014. Those with the most training and greatest amount of education, preferably a Ph.D., should find the best job prospects. Employment opportunities should be greatest in and around large metropolitan areas, where many colleges, universities, research facilities, corporations, and federal agencies are located. Individuals with statistical training will have an advantage.

FOR MORE INFORMATION

For career publications, lists of accredited schools, and job information, contact

American Sociological Association
1307 New York Avenue, NW, Suite 700
Washington, DC 20005-4712
Tel: 202-383-9005
Email: executive.office@asanet.org
http://www.asanet.org

This organization includes demographers, sociologists, economists, public health professionals, and other individuals interested in research and education in the population field. For information on job opportunities, publications, and annual conferences and workshops, contact

Population Association of America
8630 Fenton Street, Suite 722
Silver Spring, MD 20910-3812
Tel: 301-565-6710
Email: info@popassoc.org
http://www.popassoc.org

For publications, special reports, and global population information, contact

Population Reference Bureau
1875 Connecticut Avenue, NW, Suite 520
Washington, DC 20009-5728
Tel: 800-877-9881
Email: popref@prb.org
http://www.prb.org

For population statistics, as well as information on regional offices, jobs, and a calendar of events, contact

U.S. Census Bureau
4700 Silver Hill Road
Washington, DC 20233-0001
Tel: 301-763-4748
Email: recruiter@census.gov
http://www.census.gov

Desktop Publishing Designers

OVERVIEW

Desktop publishing designers prepare reports, brochures, press releases, books, cards, and other documents for printing. They create computer files of text, graphics, and page layout. They work with files others have created, or they compose original text and graphics for clients. There are approximately 34,000 desktop publishing designers employed in the United States.

HISTORY

When Johannes Gutenberg invented movable type in the 1440s, it was a major technological advancement. Up until that point, books were produced entirely by monks, every word written by hand on vellum. Though print shops flourished all across Europe with this invention, inspiring the production of millions of books by the 1500s, there was little major change in the technology of printing until the 1800s. By then, cylinder presses were churning out thousands of sheets per hour, and the Linotype machine allowed for easier, more efficient plate-making. Offset lithography (a method of applying ink from a treated surface onto paper) followed and gained popularity after World War II. Phototypesetting was later developed, involving creating film images of text and pictures to be printed. At the end of the 20th century, computers caused another revolution in the industry. Laser printers now allow for low-cost, high-quality printing, and desktop publishing software is credited with spurring sales and use of personal home computers, as well as increasing employment demand for desktop publishing designers in many industries, including public relations.

THE JOB

If you've ever used a computer to design and print a page in your high school paper or yearbook, then you've had some experience in desktop publishing. Not so many years ago, the prepress process (the steps to prepare a document for the printing press) involved metal casts, molten lead, light tables, knives, wax, paste, and a number of different professionals from artists to typesetters. With computer technology, these jobs are becoming more consolidated.

Desktop publishing designers have artistic talents, proofreading skills, sales and marketing abilities, and a great deal of computer knowledge. They work on computers converting and preparing files for printing presses and other media, such as the Internet and CD-ROM. Much of desktop publishing is called prepress, when designers typeset, or arrange and transform, text and graphics. They use the latest in design software; programs such as PhotoShop, Illustrator, InDesign, PageMaker (all from software designer Adobe), and QuarkXpress, are the most popular. Some desktop publishing designers also use CAD (computer-aided design) technology, allowing them to create images and effects with a digitizing pen.

Once they've created a file to be printed, desktop publishing designers either submit it to a commercial printer or print the pieces themselves. Whereas traditional typesetting costs over $20 per page, desktop printing can cost less than a penny a page. Individuals hire the services of desktop publishing designers for creating and printing press releases, advertising and fund-raising brochures, newsletters, flyers, and business cards. Commercial printing involves catalogs, brochures, and reports, while business printing encompasses products used by businesses, such as sales receipts and forms.

Typesetting and page layout work entails selecting font types and sizes, arranging column widths, checking for proper spacing between letters, words, and columns, placing graphics and pictures, and more. Desktop publishing designers choose from the hundreds of typefaces available, taking the purpose and tone of the text (for example, using a more informal typeface for a press release about a new youth program at the local zoo) into consideration when selecting from fonts with round shapes or long shapes, thick strokes or thin, serifs or sans serifs. Editing is also an important duty of a desktop publishing designer. Articles must be updated, or in some cases rewritten, before they are arranged on a page. As more people use their own desktop publishing programs to create print-ready files, desktop publishing designers will have to be even more skillful at designing original work and promoting their professional expertise to remain competitive.

Desktop publishing designers deal with technical issues, such as resolution problems, colors that need to be corrected, and software difficulties. A coworker may come in with a hand-drawn sketch, a printout of a design, or a file on a diskette, and he or she may want the piece ready to be posted on the Internet or to be published in a high-quality press release, brochure, newsletter, newspaper, or magazine. Each format presents different issues, and desktop publishing designers must be familiar with the processes and solutions for each. They may also provide services such as color scanning, laminating, image manipulation, and poster production.

REQUIREMENTS

High School

Classes that will help you develop desktop publishing skills include computer classes and design and art classes. Computer classes should include both hardware and software, since understanding how computers function will help you with troubleshooting and knowing a computer's limits. Through photography classes you can learn about composition, color, and design elements. Typing, drafting, and print shop classes, if available, will also provide you with the opportunity to gain some indispensable skills. Working on the school newspaper or yearbook will train you on desktop publishing skills as well, including page layout, typesetting, composition, and working under a deadline.

Postsecondary Training

Although a college degree is not a prerequisite, many desktop publishing designers have at least a bachelor's degree. Areas of study range anywhere from English to graphic design. Some two-year colleges and technical institutes offer programs in desktop publishing or related fields. A growing number of schools offer programs in technical and visual communications, which may include classes in desktop publishing, layout and design, and computer graphics. Four-year colleges also offer courses in technical communications and graphic design. You can enroll in classes related to desktop publishing through extended education programs offered through universities and colleges. These classes, often taught by professionals in the industry, cover basic desktop publishing techniques and advanced lessons on Adobe PhotoShop or QuarkXPress.

Additionally, the Association of Graphic Communications (AGC) offers an electronic publishing certificate program that covers the following topics: electronic publishing introduction, Acrobat and PDF technologies, color theory, graphic design, Illustrator, InDesign, PhotoShop,

QuarkXPress, prepress and pre-flight, print production, proofreading and copyediting, electronic publishing, scanning, and typography and font management. Contact the AGC for more information.

Other Requirements

Desktop publishing designers are detail-oriented, possess problem-solving skills, and have a sense of design and artistic skills. A good eye and patience are critical, as well as endurance to see projects through to the finish. You should have an aptitude for computers, the ability to type quickly and accurately, and a natural curiosity. In addition, a calm temperament comes in handy when working under pressure and constant deadlines. You should be flexible and be able to handle more than one project at a time.

EXPLORING

Experimenting with your home computer, or a computer at school or the library, will give you a good idea as to whether desktop publishing is for you. Play around with various graphic design and page layout programs. If you subscribe to an Internet service, take advantage of any free Web space available to you and design your own home page. Join computer clubs and volunteer to produce press releases, newsletters, and flyers for school or community clubs. Volunteering is an excellent way to try new software and techniques as well as gain experience troubleshooting and creating final products. Part-time or summer employment with printing shops and companies that have in-house publishing or printing departments are other great ways to gain experience and make valuable contacts.

EMPLOYERS

Approximately 34,000 desktop publishing designers are employed in the United States. Desktop publishing designers work for individuals and publishing houses, public relations firms, advertising agencies, graphic design agencies, and printing shops. Some large companies also contract with desktop publishing services rather than hire full-time designers. Government agencies such as the U.S. Government Printing Office hire desktop publishing designers to help produce the large number of documents they publish.

Desktop publishing designers deal directly with their clients, but in some cases they may be subcontracting work from printers, designers, and other desktop publishing designers. They may also work as consultants, working with printing professionals to help solve particular design problems.

STARTING OUT

To start your own business, you must have a great deal of experience with design and page layout, and a careful understanding of the computer design programs you'll be using. Before striking out on your own, you may want to gain experience as a full-time staff member of a large business. Most desktop publishing designers enter the field through the production side, or the editorial side of the industry. Those with training as a designer or artist can easily master the finer techniques of production. Printing houses and design agencies are places to check for production artist opportunities. Publishing companies often hire desktop publishing designers to work in-house or as freelance employees. Working within the industry, you can make connections and build up a clientele.

You can also start out by investing in computer hardware and software, and volunteering your services. By designing logos, letterhead, flyers, and press releases, for example, your work will gain quick recognition, and word of your services will spread.

ADVANCEMENT

Salaried desktop publishing designers can advance by becoming managers of other designers, being assigned larger and more involved projects, or by seeking employment at larger companies or firms.

In addition to taking on more print projects, self-employed desktop publishing designers can expand their business into Web design and page layout for Internet-based magazines or companies that desire a presence on the Web.

EARNINGS

There is limited salary information available for desktop publishing designers, most likely because the job duties of desktop publishing designer can vary and often overlap with other jobs. The average wage of desktop publishing designers in the prepress department generally ranges from $15 to $50 an hour. Entry-level desktop publishing designers with little or no experience generally earn minimum wage. Freelancers can earn from $15 to $100 an hour. According to the U.S. Department of Labor, median annual earnings of desktop publishing designers were $32,800 in 2005. The lowest 10 percent earned less than $19,190 and the highest 10 percent earned more than $53,750. Wage rates vary depending on experience, training, region, and size of the company.

WORK ENVIRONMENT

Desktop publishing designers spend most of their time working in front of a computer, whether editing text, or laying out pages. They need to be able to work with other prepress professionals, and deal with clients. Hours may vary depending on project deadlines at hand. Some projects may take just a day to complete, while others may take weeks or months. Projects range from designing a logo for letterhead, to preparing a press release for the printer, to working on a file for a company's Web site.

OUTLOOK

According to the U.S. Department of Labor, employment for desktop publishing designers is projected to grow faster than the average through 2014, even though overall employment in the printing industry is expected to decline slightly. This is due in part because electronic processes are replacing the manual processes performed by pasteup workers, photoengravers, camera operators, film strippers, and platemakers.

As technology advances, the ability to create and publish documents will become easier and faster, thus influencing more businesses to produce printed materials. Desktop publishing designers will be needed to satisfy typesetting, page layout, design, and editorial demands. With new equipment, commercial printing shops will be able to shorten the turnaround time on projects and in turn can increase business and accept more jobs. For instance, digital printing presses allow printing shops to print directly to the digital press rather than printing to a piece of film, and then printing from the film to the press. Digital printing presses eliminate an entire step and should appeal to companies that need jobs completed quickly.

QuarkXPress, Adobe PageMaker, InDesign, Macromedia Free-Hand, Adobe Illustrator, and Adobe PhotoShop are some programs often used in desktop publishing. Designers with experience in these and other software will be in demand.

FOR MORE INFORMATION

This organization is a source of financial support for education and research projects designed to promote careers in graphic communications. For more information, contact
Graphic Arts Education and Research Foundation
1899 Preston White Drive

Reston, VA 20191-5468
Tel: 866-381-9839
Email: gaerf@npes.org
http://www.gaerf.org

For industry information, contact the following organizations:
Graphic Arts Information Network
200 Deer Run Road
Sewickley, PA 15143-2324
Tel: 412-741-6860
Email: gain@piagatf.org
http://www.gain.net

National Association for Printing Leadership
75 West Century Road
Paramus, NJ 07652-1408
Tel: 800-642-6275
http://www.recouncil.org

For information on careers, student competitions, and colleges that offer training in technical communication, contact
Society for Technical Communication
901 North Stuart Street, Suite 904
Arlington, VA 22203-1822
Tel: 703-522-4114
Email: stc@stc.org
http://www.stc.org

Visit the following Web site for information on scholarships, competitions, colleges and universities that offer graphic communication programs, and careers.
GRAPHIC COMM Central
Email: gcc@teched.vt.edu
http://teched.vt.edu/gcc

Event Planners

OVERVIEW

The duties of *event planners* are varied, and may include establishing a site for an event; making travel, hotel, and food arrangements; and planning the program and overseeing the registration. The planner may be responsible for all of the negotiating, planning, and coordinating for a major worldwide convention, or the planner may be involved with a small, in-house meeting involving only a few people. Some professional associations, government agencies, corporations, nonprofit organizations, political groups, and educational institutions hire event planners or have employees on staff who have these responsibilities. Many of these organizations and companies outsource their event planning responsibilities to firms that specialize in these services, such as marketing, public relations, and event planning firms. In addition, many event and meeting planners are independent consultants.

Some event planners' services are also used on a personal level to plan class or family reunions, birthday parties, weddings, or anniversaries. There are approximately 43,000 event planners employed in the United States.

QUICK FACTS

School Subjects
Business
English
Foreign language

Personal Skills
Communication/ideas
Leadership/management

Work Environment
Primarily indoors
One location with some travel

Minimum Education Level
Bachelor's degree

Salary Range
$25,200 to $41,280 to $69,340+

Certification or Licensing
Voluntary

Outlook
Faster than the average

DOT
169

GOE
11.01.01

NOC
1226

O*NET-SOC
13-1121.00

HISTORY

According to the *National Directory of Occupational Titles and Codes,* the meeting management profession was recognized as a career in the early 1990s. As corporations have specialized and expanded their companies to include facilities and employees worldwide, the logistics of company meetings and events have become more complex. Planning a meeting that brings together employees and directors from around the world requires advanced planning to

Public Relations Industry Facts, 2004

- There were more than 7,800 public relations agencies in the United States.

- Approximately 20 percent of all public relations (PR) firms were located in California and New York.

- About 425,000 full-time workers were employed in the PR and advertising industries.

- Public relations workers averaged 33.8 hours of work per week—slightly higher than the national average of 33.7 hours for workers in all occupations.

Source: U.S. Department of Labor

acquire a site, make travel and hotel arrangements, book speakers and entertainment, and arrange for catering.

Similarly, the growth of the convention and trade show industry has resulted in the need for persons with skills specific to the planning, marketing, and execution of a successful show. Conventions, trade shows, meetings, and corporate travel have become a big business in recent years, accounting for more than $80 billion in annual spending.

The scope of meetings has changed as well. Technological advances now allow meetings to be conducted via the Internet, through videoconferencing or closed circuit television, or by setting up conference calls.

THE JOB

Event planners have a variety of duties depending on their specific title and the firm they work for or the firms they work with. Generally, planners organize and plan an event such as a meeting, a special open house, a convention, or a specific celebration.

Meetings might consist of a small interdepartmental meeting, a board meeting, an all-employee meeting, an in-house training session, a stockholders' meeting, or a meeting with vendors or distributors. When planning for these events, meeting planners usually check the calendars of key executives to establish a meeting time that fits into their schedules. Planners reserve meeting rooms, training rooms, or outside facilities for the event. They visit outside sites to make sure they are appropriate for that specific event. Planners notify people of the time, place, and date of the event and set up registration procedures, if necessary. They arrange for food, room layout, audiovisual equipment, instructors, computers, sound equipment, and telephone equipment as required.

In some cases, a company may employ an in-house meeting planner who is responsible for small- to medium-sized events. When a large meeting, trade show, conference, open house, or convention is planned, the in-house event planner may contract with outside meeting planners to assist with specific responsibilities such as registration, catering, and display setup. Some companies have their own trade show or convention managers on staff.

Convention, trade show, or *conference managers* negotiate and communicate with other enterprises related to the convention or trade show industry such as hotel and catering sales staff, speaker's bureaus, and trade staff such as *electricians* or *laborers* who set up convention display areas. They may also be responsible for contracting the transportation of the equipment and supplies to and from the event site. The manager usually works with an established budget and negotiates fees with these enterprises and enters contracts with them. Additional contracts may also need to be negotiated with professionals to handle registration, marketing, and public relations for the event.

Managers and planners need to be aware of legal aspects of trade show setups such as fire code regulations, floor plan, and space limitations, and make sure they are within these guidelines. They often need to get these arrangements approved in writing. Good record keeping and communication skills are used daily. The convention manager may have staff to handle the sales, registration, marketing, logistics, or other specific aspects of the event, or these duties may be subcontracted to another firm.

Some convention planners are employed specifically by convention and visitors' bureaus, the tourism industry, or by exhibit halls or convention facilities. Their job responsibilities may be specific to one aspect of the show, or they may be required to do any or all of the above-mentioned duties. Some convention and trade show managers may work for the exposition center or association and be responsible for selling booth space at large events.

Special event coordinators are usually employed by large corporations that hold numerous special events or by firms that contract their special event planning services to companies, associations, or religious, political, or educational groups. A special event coordinator is responsible for planning, organizing, and implementing a special event such as an open house, an anniversary, the dedication of a new facility, a special promotion or sale, an ordination, a political rally, or a victory celebration. This coordinator works with the company or organization and determines the purpose of the special event, the type of celebration desired, the site, the budget, the attendees, the food and entertainment preferences, and the anticipated outcome. The special event planner then coordinates the vendors and equipment necessary to successfully hold this event. The coordinator works closely with the client at all times to ensure that the event is being planned as expected. Follow-up assessment of the event is usually part of the services offered by the special event coordinator.

Party planners are often employed by individuals, families, or small companies to help them plan a small party for a special occasion. Many party planners are independent contractors who work out of their homes or are employees of small firms.

REQUIREMENTS

High School

If you are interested in entering the field of event planning, you should take high school classes in business, English, and speech. Because many conferences and meetings are international in scope, you may also want to take foreign language and geography courses. In addition, computer science classes will be beneficial.

Postsecondary Training

Almost all coordinators and planners must have a four-year college degree to work for a company, corporation, convention, or travel center. Some institutions offer bachelor's degrees in meeting planning; however, degrees in business, English, communications, marketing, public relations, sales, or travel would also be a good fit for a career as a meetings manager, convention planner, or special event coordinator. Many directors and planners who become company heads have earned graduate degrees.

Some small firms, convention centers, or exhibit facilities may accept persons with associate's degrees or travel industry certification for certain planning positions. Party planners may not always need education beyond high school, but advancement opportunities will be more plentiful with additional education.

Certification or Licensing

There are some professional associations for planners that offer certification programs. For example, Meeting Professionals International offers the certification in meeting management designation.

The International Association of Exhibitions and Events offers the certified in exhibition management designation. The Convention Industry Council offers the certified meeting professional designation. (See "For More Information" at the end of this article for contact information for these organizations.)

Other Requirements

To be an event planner, you must have excellent organizational skills, the ability to plan projects and events, and the ability to think creatively. You must be able to work well with people and anticipate their needs in advance. You should be willing to pitch in to get a job done even though it may not be part of your duties. In a situation where there is an unforeseen crisis, you need to react quickly and professionally. Planners should have good negotiating and communication skills and be assertive but tactful.

EXPLORING

High school guidance counselors can supply information on event planners or convention coordinators. Public and school librarians may also be able to provide useful books, magazines, and pamphlets. Searching the Internet for companies that provide event-planning services can give you an idea of the types of services that they offer. Professional associations related to the travel, convention, and meeting industries may have career information available to students. Some of these organizations are listed at the end of this article.

Attending local trade shows and conventions will provide insight into the operations of this industry. Also, some exhibit and convention halls may hire students to assist with various aspects of trade show operations. You can learn more about this profession by subscribing to magazines such as *Meetings & Conventions* (http://www.meetings-conventions.com).

Some party planners may hire assistants to help with children's birthday parties or other special events. Organize and plan a large family event, such as a birthday, anniversary, graduation, or retirement celebration. You will have to find a location, hire caterers or assign family members to bring specific food items, send invitations, purchase and arrange decorations, and organize entertainment, all according to what your budget allows.

You can also gain business experience through school activities. Join the business club, run for student council, or head the prom committee to learn how to plan and carry out events.

EMPLOYERS

Many large corporations or institutions worldwide hire meeting managers, convention managers, or event planners to handle their specific activities. Although some companies may not have employees with the specific title of event planner or meeting manager, these skills are very marketable and these duties may be part of another job title. In many companies, these duties may be part of a position within the marketing, public relations, or corporate communications department.

Convention facilities, exhibit halls, training and educational institutions, travel companies, and health care facilities also hire event planners. Hotels often hire planners to handle meetings and events held within their facilities. Large associations usually maintain an event planning staff for one or more annual conventions or business meetings for their members.

Job opportunities are also available with companies that contract out event and meeting planning services. Many of these companies have positions that specialize in certain aspects of the planning service, such as travel coordinator, exhibit planner, facilities negotiator, or they have people who perform specific functions such as trade show display setup, registration, and follow-up reporting.

Planners interested in jobs with the convention and trade show industries or hotels may find that larger cities have more demand for planners and offer higher salaries.

Experienced meeting planners or convention managers may choose to establish their own businesses or independently contract out their services. Party planning may also be a good independent business venture. Approximately 43,000 event planners are employed in the United States.

STARTING OUT

An internship at a visitors and convention bureau, exhibit center, or with a travel agency or meeting planning company is a good way to meet and network with other people in this field. Attending trade shows might offer a chance to speak with people about the field and to discuss any contacts they might have.

Some colleges and universities may offer job placement for people seeking careers in meeting planning or in the convention and trade show industries. Professional associations related to these industries are also good contacts for someone starting out. Classified ads and trade magazines may also offer some job leads.

ADVANCEMENT

Advancement opportunities for people in the event planning field are good. Experienced planners can expect to move into positions of increased responsibility. They may become senior managers and executive directors of private businesses, hotels, convention facilities, exhibit halls, travel corporations, museums, or other facilities. They can advance within a corporation to a position with more responsibilities or they may go into the planning business for themselves. Planners who have established a good reputation in the industry are often recruited by other firms or facilities and can advance their careers with these opportunities.

EARNINGS

According to the U.S. Department of Labor, meeting and convention planners earned median annual salaries of $41,280 in 2005. The lowest 10 percent earned less than $25,200, and the highest 10 percent earned more than $69,340.

Benefits may vary depending on the position and the employer but generally include vacation, sick leave, insurance, and other work-related benefits.

WORK ENVIRONMENT

Work environments vary with the planner's title and job responsibilities, but generally planners can expect to work in a business setting as part of a team. Usually, the planner's initial planning work is done in a clean environment with modern equipment prior to the opening of a convention or trade show. Working in convention and trade show environments, however, can be noisy, crowded, and distracting. In addition, the days can be long and may require standing for hours. If the planner is involved with supervising the setup or dismantling of a trade show or convention, the work can be dirty and physically demanding.

Although most facilities have crews that assist with setup, meeting planners occasionally get involved with last-minute changes and may need to do some physical lifting of equipment, tables, or chairs.

Event planners can usually expect to work erratic hours, often putting in long days prior to the event and the day the event is actually held. Travel is often part of the job requirements and may include working and/or traveling nights and on the weekends.

OUTLOOK

Job opportunities for event planners will continue to grow at a faster-than-average rate through 2014, according to the U.S. Department of Labor. The introduction of new technology enables more meetings to take place than ever before. Conventions, trade shows, meetings, and incentive travel support more than 1.5 million American jobs, according to the Professional Convention Management Association. These events account for more than $80 billion in annual spending.

FOR MORE INFORMATION

For information on certification, contact
Convention Industry Council
1620 I Street, NW, 6th Floor
Washington, DC 20006-4005
Tel: 202-429-8634
http://www.conventionindustry.org

For information on careers in the field of event planning, contact the following organizations.
International Association of Exhibitions and Events
PO Box 802425
Dallas, TX 75380-2425
Tel: 972-458-8002
http://www.iaee.com

Meeting Professionals International
3030 Lyndon B. Johnson Freeway, Suite 1700
Dallas, TX 75234-2759
Tel: 972-702-3000
Email: feedback@mpiweb.org
http://www.mpiweb.org

Professional Convention Management Association
2301 South Lake Shore Drive, Suite 1001
Chicago, IL 60616-1419
Tel: 312-423-7262
Email: students@pcma.org
http://www.pcma.org

Media Planners and Buyers

OVERVIEW

Media specialists are responsible for placing advertisements that will reach targeted customers and get the best response from the market for the least amount of money. Within the media department, *media planners* gather information about the sizes and types of audiences that can be reached through each of the various media and about the cost of advertising in each medium. *Media buyers,* sometimes called *advertising sales agents,* purchase space in printed publications, as well as time on radio or television stations. Advertising media workers are supervised by a *media director,* who is accountable for the overall media plan. In addition to advertising agencies, media planners and buyers work for large companies that purchase space or broadcast time. There are approximately 154,000 advertising sales agents employed in the United States.

HISTORY

The first formal media that allowed advertisers to deliver messages about their products or services to the public were newspapers and magazines, which began selling space to advertisers in the late 19th century. This system of placing ads gave rise to the first media planners and buyers, who were in charge of deciding what kind of advertising to put in which publications and then actually purchasing the space.

In the broadcast realm, radio stations started offering program time to advertisers in the early 1900s. And, while television

QUICK FACTS

School Subjects
Business
English
Speech

Personal Skills
Artistic
Communication/ideas

Work Environment
Primarily indoors
One location with some
   travel

Minimum Education Level
Bachelor's degree

Salary Range
$18,000 to $43,910 to
   $120,000+

Certification or Licensing
None available

Outlook
Faster than the average

DOT
162

GOE
11.09.01

NOC
1225

O*NET-SOC
41-3011.00

Media planners and buyers must have experience with both database and word processing. *(The Image Works)*

advertising began just before the end of World War II, producers were quick to realize that they could reach huge audiences by placing ads on TV. Television advertising proved to be beneficial to the TV stations as well, since they relied on sponsors for financial assistance in order to bring programs into people's homes. In the past, programs were sometimes named not for the host or star of the program, but for the sponsoring company that was paying for the broadcast of that particular show.

During the early years of radio and television, it was often possible for one sponsor to pay for an entire 30-minute program. The cost of producing shows on radio and television, however, increased dramatically, requiring many sponsors to support a single radio or television program. Media planners and buyers learned to get more for their money by buying smaller amounts of time—60-, 30-, and even 10-second spots—on a greater number of programs.

Today's media planners and buyers have a wide array of media from which to choose. The newest of these, the World Wide Web, allows advertisers not only to precisely target customers but to interact with them as well. In addition to Web banner ads, producers can also advertise via sponsorships, their own Web sites, CD catalogs, voice-mail telephone shopping, and more. With so many choices, media planners and buyers must carefully determine target markets and select the ideal media mix in order to reach these markets at the least cost.

THE JOB

While many employees may work in the media department, the primary specialists are the media planner and the media buyer. They work with professionals from a wide range of media—from billboards, direct mail, and newspapers and magazines to television, radio, and the Internet. Both types of media specialists must be familiar with the markets that each medium reaches, as well as the advantages and disadvantages of advertising in each.

Media planners determine target markets based on their clients' advertising approaches. Considering their clients' products and services, budget, and image, media planners gather information about the public's viewing, reading, and buying habits by administering questionnaires and conducting other forms of market research. Through this research, planners are able to identify target markets by sorting data according to people's ages, incomes, marital status, interests, and leisure activities.

By knowing which groups of people read particular magazines or newspapers, for example, media planners can help clients select airtime or print space to reach the consumers most likely to buy their products. For example, television or radio news shows often attract those who are interested in current events. For shows broadcast at this time, media planners will recommend airtime to their clients who are interested in advertising a newspaper such as the *New York Times* or *Chicago Tribune* to these viewers. Media planners who work directly for companies selling airtime or print space must be sensitive to their clients' budgets and resources. When tailoring their sales pitch to a particular client's needs, planners often go to great lengths to persuade the client to buy airtime or advertising space. They produce brochures and reports that detail the characteristics of their viewing or reading market, including the average income of those individuals, the number of people who see the ads, and any other information that may be likely to encourage potential advertisers to promote their products.

Media planners try to land contracts by inviting clients to meetings and presentations and educating them about various marketing strategies. They must not only pursue new clients but also attend to current ones, making sure that they are happy with their existing advertising packages. For both new and existing clients, the media planner's main objective is to sell as much airtime or ad space as possible.

Media buyers do the actual purchasing of the time on radio or television or the space in a newspaper or magazine in which an advertisement will run. In addition to tracking the time and space available for purchase, media buyers ensure that ads appear when and where they should, negotiate costs for ad placement, and calculate rates, usage, and budgets. They are also responsible for maintaining contact with clients, keeping them informed of all advertising-related developments and resolving any conflicts that arise. Large companies that generate a lot of advertising or those that place only print ads or only broadcast ads sometimes differentiate between the two main media groups by employing *space buyers* and/or *time buyers.*

Workers who actually sell the print space or airtime to advertisers are called *print sales workers* or *broadcast time salespeople.* Like media planners, these professionals are well versed about the target markets served by their organizations and can often provide useful information about editorial content or broadcast programs.

In contrast to print and broadcast planners and buyers, *interactive media specialists* are responsible for managing all critical aspects of their clients' online advertising campaigns. While interactive media planners may have responsibilities similar to those of print or broadcast planners, they also act as new technology specialists, placing and tracking all online ads and maintaining relationships with clients and Webmasters alike.

The typical online media planning process begins with an agency spreadsheet that details the criteria about the media buy. These criteria often include target demographics, start and end dates for the ad campaign, and online objectives. After sending all relevant information to a variety of Web sites, the media specialist receives cost, market, and other data from the sites. Finally, the media specialist places the order and sends all creative information needed to the selected Web sites. Once the order has been placed, the media specialist receives tracking and performance data and then compiles and analyzes the information in preparation for future ad campaigns.

Media planners and buyers may have a wide variety of clients. Magazine and newspaper publishers, film studios, television networks, restaurants, hotel chains, beverage companies, food product manufacturers, and automobile dealers all need to advertise to attract potential customers. While huge companies, such as motion picture studios, soft drink manufacturers, major airlines, and vacation resorts, pay a lot of money to have their products or services advertised nationally, many smaller firms need to advertise only in their immediate area. Local advertising may come from a health club that wants to announce a special membership rate or from a retail store promoting a sale. Media planners and buyers must be aware of their various clients' advertising needs and create campaigns that will accomplish their promotional objectives.

REQUIREMENTS

High School

Although most media positions, including those at the entry level, require a bachelor's degree, you can prepare for a future job as media planner and/or buyer by taking specific courses offered at the high school level. These include business, marketing, advertising, cinematography, radio and television, and film and video. General liberal arts classes, such as economics, English, communication, and journalism, are also important, since media planners and buyers must be able to communicate clearly with both clients and coworkers. In addition, mathematics classes will give you the skills to work accurately with budget figures and placement costs.

Postsecondary Training

Increasingly, media planners and buyers have college degrees, often with majors in marketing or advertising. Even if you have prior work experience or training in media, you should select college classes that provide a good balance of business course work, broadcast and print experience, and liberal arts studies.

Business classes may include economics, marketing, sales, and advertising. In addition, courses that focus on specific media, such as cinematography, film and video, radio and television, and new technologies (like the Internet), are important. Additional classes in journalism, English, and speech will prove helpful as well. Media directors often need to have a master's degree, as well as extensive experience working with the various media.

Other Requirements

Media planners and buyers in broadcasting should have a keen understanding of programming and consumer buying trends, as well as a knowledge of each potential client's business. Print media specialists must be familiar with the process involved in creating print ads and the markets reached by various publications. In addition, all media workers need to be capable of maintaining good relationships with current clients, as well as pursuing new clients on a continual basis.

Communication and problem-solving skills are important, as are creativity, common sense, patience, and persistence. Media planners and buyers must also have excellent oral, written, and analytical skills, knowledge of interactive media planning trends and tools, and the ability to handle multiple assignments in a fast-paced work environment. Strategic thinking skills, industry interest, and computer experience with both database and word processing programs are also vital.

EXPLORING

Many high schools and two-year colleges and most four-year colleges have media departments that may include radio stations and public access or cable television channels. In order to gain worthwhile experience in media, you can work for these departments as aides, production assistants, programmers, or writers. In addition, high school and college newspapers and yearbooks often need students to sell advertising to local merchants. Theater departments also frequently look for people to sell ads for performance programs.

In the local community, newspapers and other publications often hire high school students to work part time and/or in the summer in sales and clerical positions for the classified advertising department. Some towns have cable television stations that regularly look for volunteers to operate cameras, sell advertising, and coordinate various programs. In addition, a variety of religious-sponsored activities, such as craft fairs, holiday boutiques, and rummage sales, can provide you with opportunities to create and place ads and work with the local media in order to get exposure for the events.

EMPLOYERS

Media planners and buyers often work for advertising agencies in large cities, such as Chicago, New York, and Los Angeles. These agencies represent various clients who are trying to sell everything from financial services to dishwasher soap to the latest comedy featuring the hot star of the moment. Other media specialists work directly for radio and television networks, newspapers, magazines, and Web sites selling airtime and print space. While many of these media organizations are located in large urban areas, particularly radio and television stations, most small towns put out newspapers and therefore need specialists to sell ad space and coordinate accounts. Approximately 154,000 advertising sales agents work in the United States. Thirty percent of agents work in newspaper, book, and directory publishing.

STARTING OUT

More than half of the jobs in print and broadcast media do not remain open long enough for companies to advertise available positions in the classified sections of newspapers. As a result, many media organizations, such as radio and television stations, do not usually advertise job openings in the want ads. Media planners and buyers often hear about available positions through friends, acquaintances, or family members and frequently enter the field as entry-level broadcasting or sales associates. Both broadcasting and sales can provide employees just starting out with experience in approaching and working for clients, as well as knowledge about the specifics of programming and its relation to selling airtime.

Advertising agencies sometimes do advertise job openings, both in local and national papers and on the Web. Competition is quite fierce for entry-level jobs, however, particularly at large agencies in big cities.

Print media employees often start working on smaller publications as in-house sales staff members, answering telephones and taking orders from customers. Other duties may include handling classified ads or coordinating the production and placement of small print ads created by in-house artists. While publications often advertise for entry-level positions, the best way to find work in advertising is to send resumes to as many agencies, publications, and broadcasting offices as possible. With any luck, your resume will arrive just as an opening is becoming available.

While you are enrolled in a college program, you should investigate opportunities for internships or on-campus employment in related areas. Your school's career planning center or placement office should have information on such positions. Previous experience often provides a competitive edge for all job seekers, but it is crucial to aspiring media planners and buyers.

ADVANCEMENT

Large agencies and networks often hire only experienced people, so it is common for media planners and buyers to learn the business at smaller companies. These opportunities allow media specialists to gain the experience and confidence they need to move up to more advanced positions. Jobs at smaller agencies and television and radio stations also provide possibilities for more rapid promotion than those at larger organizations.

Media planners and buyers climbing the company ladder can advance to the position of media director or may earn promotions to executive-level positions. For those already at the management level, advancement can come in the form of larger clients and more responsibility. In addition, many media planners and buyers who have experience with traditional media are investigating the opportunities and challenges that come with the job of interactive media planner/buyer or *Web media specialist.*

EARNINGS

Because media planners and buyers work for a variety of organizations all across the country and abroad, earnings can vary greatly. Media directors can earn between $46,000 and $118,400, depending on the type of employer and the director's experience level. For example, directors at small agencies make an average of $42,100, while those at large agencies can earn more than $120,000, according to a 2002 *Advertising Age* salary survey.

Media planners and buyers in television typically earn higher salaries than those in radio. In general, however, beginning broadcasting salespeople usually earn between $18,000 and $35,000 per year and can advance to as much as $46,000 after a few years of experience.

According to the U.S. Department of Labor, advertising sales agents had salaries that ranged from less than $21,080 to more than $89,710 in 2005. Advertising sales agents employed in the newspaper, book, and directory publishing had mean annual earnings of $43,910 in 2005.

Most employers of media planners and buyers offer a variety of benefits, including health and life insurance, a retirement plan, and paid vacation and sick days.

WORK ENVIRONMENT

Although media planners and buyers often work a 40-hour week, their hours are not strictly nine to five. Service calls, presentations, and meetings with ad space reps and clients are important parts of the job that usually have a profound effect on work schedules. In addition, media planners and buyers must invest considerable time investigating and reading about trends in programming, buying, and advertising.

The variety of opportunities for media planners and buyers results in a wide diversity of working conditions. Larger advertising agencies, publications, and networks may have modern and comfortable working facilities. Smaller markets may have more modest working environments.

Whatever the size of the organization, many planners seldom go into the office and must call in to keep in touch with the home organization. Travel is a big part of media planners' responsibilities to their clients, and they may have clients in many different types of businesses and services, as well as in different areas of the country.

While much of the media planner and buyer's job requires interaction with a variety of people, including coworkers, sales reps, supervisors, and clients, most media specialists also perform many tasks that require independent work, such as researching and writing reports. In any case, the media planner and buyer must be able to handle many tasks at the same time in a fast-paced, continually changing environment.

OUTLOOK

The employment outlook for media planners and buyers, like the outlook for the advertising industry itself, depends on the general health of the economy. When the economy thrives, companies produce an increasing number of goods and seek to promote them via newspapers, magazines, television, radio, the Internet, and various other media. The U.S. Department of Labor anticipates that employment in the advertising industry is projected to grow 22 percent over the 2004-14 period, faster than the average for all industries.

More and more people are relying on radio and television for their entertainment and information. With cable and local television channels offering a wide variety of programs, advertisers are increasingly turning to TV in order to get exposure for their products and services. Although newspaper sales are in decline, there is growth in special interest periodicals and other print publications. Interactive media, such as the Internet, CD catalogs, and voice-mail shopping, are providing a flurry of advertising activity all around the world. All of this activity will increase market opportunities for media planners and buyers.

Employment possibilities for media specialists are far greater in large cities, such as New York, Los Angeles, and Chicago, where most magazines and many broadcast networks have their headquarters. However, smaller publications are often located in outlying areas, and large national organizations usually have sales offices in several cities across the country.

Competition for all advertising positions, including entry-level jobs, is expected to be intense. Media planners and buyers who have considerable experience will have the best chances of finding employment.

FOR MORE INFORMATION

For information on college chapters, internship opportunities, and financial aid opportunities, contact
American Advertising Federation
1101 Vermont Avenue, NW, Suite 500
Washington, DC 20005-6306
Tel: 202-898-0089
Email: aaf@aaf.org
http://www.aaf.org

For information on advertising agencies, contact
American Association of Advertising Agencies
405 Lexington Avenue, 18th Floor
New York, NY 10174-1801
Tel: 212-682-2500
http://www.aaaa.org

For career resources and job listings, contact
American Marketing Association
311 South Wacker Drive, Suite 5800
Chicago, IL 60606-6629
Tel: 800-262-1150
Email: info@ama.org
http://www.marketingpower.com

For information on education and training, contact
Marketing Research Association
110 National Drive, 2nd Floor
Glastonbury, CT 06033-1212
Tel: 860-682-1000
Email: email@mra-net.org
http://www.mra-net.org

Media Relations Specialists

OVERVIEW

Media relations specialists are experienced *public relations specialists* who have a broad working knowledge of television, radio, and print journalism and skills in establishing a controlled, positive image in the media for a company, person, or organization. They are also referred to as *communications consultants*. Media relations specialists serve as the liaison between the company, person, or organization they represent and newspaper, magazine, and broadcast news editors and reporters. The number of people working in media relations and their locations falls within the same parameters as public relations specialists. There are approximately 188,000 public relations specialists employed in the United States.

HISTORY

Similar to public relations, media relations is rooted in the 19th century, when newspapers began running positive articles about businesses that advertised in the paper to encourage future advertising. By the early 20th century, literary bureaus were established to contrive these articles, and publicity agents began surfacing in large cities. However, the articles began to undermine the newspapers' objectivity, and the practice was soon halted in the United States.

But the link between media relations and newspapers endured through reporters who were willing to use language's effects on public image to present a company or organization in a positive light. By the end of World War II, government agencies and politicians

QUICK FACTS

School Subjects
Business
English
Speech

Personal Skills
Communication/ideas
Leadership/management

Work Environment
Primarily indoors
Primarily one location

Minimum Education Level
Bachelor's degree

Salary Range
$26,870 to $45,020 to $84,300+

Certification or Licensing
Voluntary

Outlook
Faster than the average

DOT
165

GOE
01.03.01

NOC
0611

O*NET-SOC
27-3031.00

A media relations specialist is surrounded by journalists as she prepares to make a statement regarding her client. *(Corbis)*

followed business's example by hiring public relations specialists to help deliver information to the press and to advise them on their appearances at press conferences and interviews.

Media relations is now an essential function of public relations. Virtually every public relations agency either employs media relations specialists or assigns media relations duties for each client to account executives. Likewise, most large companies and organizations have someone in charge of media relations.

THE JOB

As Wendy Leinhart, media specialist with Marcy Monyak & Associates in Chicago, emphasizes, "Media relations is not a stand-alone job; it is a function of public relations." In other words, media relations is just one, but perhaps the most significant, part of public relations.

Media relations specialists develop corporate or product positioning strategies for specific media outlets; plan photo and editorial opportunities for use in the media and develop editorial ideas to fit a publication's or broadcast medium's special promotions; develop news and feature releases and pitch them to the media; place articles with the media; gain favorable product reviews and publicize them to the media; position the organization they represent as an expert source; execute media events, such as press conferences, interviews, tours, and promotions; handle information requests from the press; and collect and analyze media coverage of the organization they represent.

To understand the media relations specialist's work, suppose a large pharmaceutical company has to recall one of its products because of possible tampering. The company's Chief Executtive Officer decides she wants to address the issue with the public. The media relations specialist decides between arranging a press conference or an interview with a newspaper journalist from a major newspaper, contacts the appropriate media (in the case of a press conference) or reporter (in the case of an interview), and then briefs the CEO as to the angles on which the reporter or reporters will be basing questions.

Successful media relations depends on building an authentic rapport with reporters and editors while giving them something they can use. Media relations specialists are aware that most reliable journalists despise news that originates with a public relations slant, but that journalists often must rely on it because of time constraints. This is the reason rapport-building skills are essential in media relations.

Because the press release is at the heart of media relations, and major newspapers and wire services receive thousands of releases per day, the experienced media relations specialist knows when something is actually newsworthy and presents it in the most concise, attractive, and easy-to-read manner as possible.

REQUIREMENTS

High School

While your overall schedule should be college preparatory, there are a number of classes you should emphasize during your high school career. Naturally, English and communication classes, such as speech or debate, should be a top priority as they will help you hone your communication skills. Also, take computer classes and other classes that emphasize working with different media, such as radio or television broadcasting classes and journalism classes. Courses in mathematics, economics, and business will help you develop the skills you will need to work with budgets and project planning. If your high school offers advertising or marketing classes, be sure to take those. Finally, since a media relations specialist is involved with current events, take any history or social studies class that emphasizes this subject. Such a class will give you the opportunity to observe how current events are related to the public through different media and the influences these media can have.

Postsecondary Training

To become a media relations specialist, you should have at least a bachelor's degree in communications, public relations, or journalism. Many college programs require or encourage their students to complete internships in public relations, either during the school year or the summer. These internships often provide valuable hands-on experience. Typical classes for those majoring in public relations include public relations management; writing courses that cover news releases, speeches, and proposals; and visual communications such as computer graphics. Other courses you should take include psychology, sociology, and business administration. A master's degree may be helpful as you advance in your career.

Certification or Licensing

Although certification or licensing are not required, you may find it beneficial to get accreditation in the communications field. The Public Relations Society of America accredits public relations professionals who have at least five years of experience with the accredited in public relations designation, which can be obtained by passing a written and oral examination. The International Association of Business Communicators also offers the accredited business communicator designation.

Other Requirements

In addition to excellent verbal and written communication skills, you need to be creative and aggressive, coming up with new and appealing ideas to attract media interest in your clients. You also need to be able to work under the pressure of deadlines, be able to make decisions quickly and effectively, and do thorough research. In addition, as a media relations specialist, you should have an interest in continuously learning about new technologies and using these new technologies to promote the interests of your clients.

EXPLORING

During your high school years, become involved with the school newspaper, yearbook, or literary magazine. Try working with these publications' advertising departments or sections, either selling ad space or promoting the publication to the student body. You can also join school committees that plan and publicize events such as school dances, fund-raisers, or other functions. Try your hand at other media by working at the school television or radio station. You may even be able to come up with your own ad campaign for a school event.

The best way to explore this career during your college years is to complete an internship at a public relations firm. If you are unable to get such an internship, try getting a part-time or summer job at a local newspaper, radio, or television station where you can work in some type of public relations department. Read publications by the Public Relations Society of America (http://www.prsa.org/publications), such as *The Strategist* and *Public Relations Tactics,* to become more familiar with how the public relations field works.

EMPLOYERS

Media relations specialists are employed either by the organization, company, or individual they represent or by a public relations agency. The majority of opportunities exist in major metropolitan areas, but there also may be opportunities even in smaller communities, such as at colleges and universities. Approximately 188,000 public relations managers are employed in the United States.

STARTING OUT

It is not likely that you'll begin your career in media relations right after graduating from college. Even someone with a professional journalism background should not jump into media relations without first working as a public relations generalist. "Most media relations specialists work entry-level PR jobs after working as a journalist, and fall into media relations as a specialty," Wendy Leinhart says. Also important is computer literacy, as the proliferation of online services continues.

College career services counselors can help you find a position that will prepare you for media relations. Other effective routes include completing an internship at a public relations agency or in a corporate public relations or communications department.

ADVANCEMENT

Entry-level public relations specialists might assemble media clippings or create media lists for different clients. As they gain experience, they may be assigned to write news releases, conduct a poll or survey, or write speeches for company officials.

As prospective media relations specialists become more experienced and knowledgeable about the organization they represent, they may be called on to help seasoned media relations specialists pitch news releases, place articles with the media, and plan media events.

Seasoned media relations specialists can move into managerial positions where they take an active role in shaping media strategies and positioning the organization they represent.

EARNINGS

The U.S. Department of Labor reports that the lowest paid 10 percent of public relations specialists made approximately $26,870 or less in 2005, while the highest paid 10 percent earned $84,300 or more. Salaried public relations specialists earned an average of $45,020 in 2005.

Media relations specialists working for consulting firms, agencies, and large corporations earn the most, while those in the nonprofit sector earn less.

Media relations specialists receive standard benefits, including health insurance, paid vacations, and sick days. They also receive regular salary increases and are often given expense accounts.

WORK ENVIRONMENT

Media relations specialists usually work in a traditional office environment and work between 40 and 50 hours per week. From time to time, tight project deadlines may call for more overtime than usual. Media relations specialists are expected to be tastefully dressed and socially poised and to maintain a professional demeanor. Often, they must entertain editors and reporters at lunches or dinners. Frequently, their conduct in their personal life is important if they are employed by a public relations agency or as a consultant to a client. Media relations specialists also are required to travel from time to time for business.

OUTLOOK

Competition among corporations continues to grow, as does the competition for funding between nonprofit organizations. In addition, individuals in the public eye, such as politicians and sports figures, continue to want expert advice on shaping their images. Thus, public relations will remain among the fastest-growing fields, and media relations as a component of public relations will continue to grow. The U.S. Department of Labor predicts that employment for public relations specialists will grow faster than the average for all occupations through 2014.

Competition for media relations positions will be stiff because, as with public relations, so many job seekers are enticed by the perceived glamour and appeal of the field. However, those with journalism backgrounds will have an advantage.

FOR MORE INFORMATION

For information on certification and Communications World *magazine, contact*
International Association of Business Communicators
One Halladie Plaza, Suite 600
San Francisco, CA 94102-2842
Tel: 415-544-4700
Email: service_centre@iabc.com
http://www.iabc.com

For career, certification, and student membership information, contact
Public Relations Society of America
Career Information
33 Maiden Lane, 11th Floor
New York, NY 10038-5150
Tel: 212-460-1400
Email: prssa@prsa.org (student membership)
http://www.prsa.org

For information on program accreditation and professional development, contact
Canadian Public Relations Society Inc.
4195 Dundas Street West, Suite 346
Toronto, ON M8X 1Y4 Canada
Tel: 416-239-7034
Email: admin@cprs.ca
http://www.cprs.ca

Personal Stylists and Image Consultants

OVERVIEW

Personal stylists advise clients regarding their manner of dress in order to portray an image that is appropriate for their position and employer. Most stylists work on a consulting basis, dealing with clients from a variety of industries such as banking, public relations, advertising, politics, and entertainment.

Image consultants help people and organizations present themselves in a professional manner. Image consultants offer programs for individual women or men, for professional or social organizations, or for all the employees of a single company.

HISTORY

Businesses and individuals have long used public relations to help them achieve visibility and name recognition, which in turn led to professional success. Public relations specialists often worked on a client's first impression, be it from a fellow colleague, competitor, shareholder, or customer. Many times clients were coached on how to behave, speak, and dress in public. Personal styling and image consulting emerged as public relations specialties as more and more clients expressed a desire to dress and act for success.

QUICK FACTS

School Subjects
Art
Business

Personal Skills
Artistic
Communication/ideas

Work Environment
Primarily indoors
Primarily multiple locations

Minimum Education Level
Some postsecondary training

Salary Range
$15,000 to $40,000 to $100,000+

Certification or Licensing
Recommended

Outlook
About as fast as the average

DOT
N/A

GOE
N/A

NOC
6481

O*NET-SOC
N/A

THE JOB

In the corporate world, part of your success hinges on the image you convey to your business associates and staff, as well as the competition. The way you dress can suggest your degree of ability, trustworthiness, confidence, and even serve as a measure of your economic status or educational level. For this reason, many business executives often retain the services of a personal stylist to fine-tune their corporate image.

Consultation with a personal stylist may take one session or more, depending on the extent of the makeover. A typical session lasts approximately two to four hours. The personal stylist's first step is to research the client's industry and position within the company. A personal stylist will also address the company's brand and the office culture in order to gain a clear picture of the needs of the client. For conservative industries, such as finance or accounting, the stylist may suggest a more subdued look. Stylists might suggest a more casual—yet professional—look for workers in industries such as publishing or advertising, which tend to feature more relaxed work-places. Many offices have instituted "casual Friday" or "business casual" days in which employees are encouraged to dress in a more casual manner. This has led to different interpretations of casual clothing, some unprofessional or distracting to other employees. Stylists can recommend a look that is pared down, yet appropriate to the business and position.

Wardrobe analysis is the next step. The stylist assesses articles of clothing already owned by the client, and offers advice on additional clothing or accessories to purchase. Oftentimes, a personal shopping service is included in the consultation. Stylists will also advise their client on the best suit or dress to wear for special functions such as annual meetings, press conferences, televised interviews, charitable events, or formal galas. They may also refer the client to other image experts such as image consultants, trainers and dieticians, voice or dialect coaches, and hair and make-up artists so that their client can remake his or her entire image, if necessary.

Personal stylists do not only work with business executives. Some newly promoted employees may turn to the expertise of stylists to help them update their work wardrobe to reflect their new position. Some stylists are hired to work with an entire department that has more visibility or contact with the public. For example, a bank may use stylists to coach their customer representatives or personal bank-ers regarding choices of dress, hair, makeup, and jewelry to portray a professional image. Stylists may work with the wait staff and other front-of-the-house employees of an upscale restaurant to create an image that mirrors the theme or atmosphere of the establishment. Stylists often help new college graduates change their look from col-legiate to a more professional approach. Politicians, athletes, enter-tainers, and television personalities also rely on stylists to polish their look in hopes of appearing more favorable to the public.

Image consultants help people bring out their best personal and professional presence. Susan Fignar, president of S. Fignar & Associates Inc., is a corporate image trainer and consultant who has been quoted in *Cosmopolitan,* the *Wall Street Journal,* and the *Chicago Tribune.* She works with some of the country's largest corporations and offers a variety of corporate programs and interactive workshops. Her training sessions deal with such topics as making a good first impression, everyday etiquette, developing self-esteem and confidence, verbal communication, body language and facial expression, overall appearance, and appropriate dress for every occasion. She notices an increasing demand for her services in dress code consulting and training sessions on business casual dress.

Most personal stylists and image consultants are entrepreneurs, meaning that they own and manage their businesses and assume all the risks. They may work with individuals, groups, or both. Like other entrepreneurs, their business requires constant sales and marketing to obtain clients.

REQUIREMENTS

High School

If you are interested in this work, you will benefit from taking classes and being involved in activities that develop your ability to communicate and increase your understanding of visual effects. Helpful classes include English, speech, and drama. Activities to consider participating in include drama clubs and debate teams. In drama club you may have the opportunity to help apply makeup, select wardrobes, and learn about the emotional impact appearance and behaviors can have. Art classes are also helpful to take, especially classes that teach color theory. Since many people in this line of work are entrepreneurs, consider taking business, bookkeeping, and accounting classes, which will give you the skills to run your own business.

Any part-time job working with the public is valuable. You can gain excellent experience from selling clothing or cosmetics in department stores, from working in beauty salons or spas, or from working as waitpersons. Volunteer work that involves working with people will also help you hone your people skills.

Postsecondary Training

There are no formal, standardized training programs for personal stylists and image consultants. In general, Susan Fignar recommends attending seminars or classes on color, psychology, training methods, and communications. She adds that a degree in liberal arts, with a major in education, is a plus for those working at the corporate level.

If you get to know a personal stylist or image consultant personally, you may be able to arrange an informal internship of your own. Some people begin their careers in this field by working as apprentices to stylists and consultants.

Certification or Licensing
The Association of Image Consultants International (AICI) provides three levels of certification: first level certification, certified image professional, and certified image master. Contact the AICI for more information.

Other Requirements
A general flair for art and design would prove useful for those interested in these careers. Stylists and consultants should be friendly, outgoing, supportive of others, able to offer constructive feedback, and open to change. There are few disabilities that would prevent an individual from doing this work.

Susan Fignar believes experience in the business world, especially in management and public contact, is essential for corporate consulting. She says that corporate consultants must be mature, poised, and professional to have credibility, and that people are usually between the ages of 33 and 40 when they enter this field.

EXPLORING

One way to explore this career is to arrange for a personal visit to a stylist or consultant. The AICI, for example, offers lists of qualified consultants throughout the country (see the end of this article for contact information).

There are several books you can read to learn more about style and image consulting. Susan Fignar recommends *Image Consulting: The New Career* by Joan Timberlake (Acropolis Books, 1983), which discusses the various areas in which image consultants specialize. Because networking is so important in getting clients, she also suggests *Networlding: Building Relationships and Opportunities for Success* by Melissa Giovagnoli and Jocelyn Carter-Miller (John Wiley & Sons, 2001). Local libraries should have additional books on color, fabrics, style, etiquette, and body language.

EMPLOYERS

For the most part, personal stylists and image consultants are self-employed. They run their own consulting businesses, which allows them the freedom to decide what services they wish to offer. For example, some stylists and consultants concentrate on working with corporate clients; others may also advise individuals. Those in apprenticeships and consultants just entering the field may work for stylists and consultants who have already established their businesses.

STARTING OUT

Some consultants enter the field through apprenticeships. Susan Fignar began by working in advertising, where she had extensive experience in meeting planning and often was responsible for company visitors. She eventually attended a training program on fashion and image consulting. She says there are many routes to enter this field.

ADVANCEMENT

Susan Fignar hopes to expand her business by adding new clients, taking advantage of new trends, developing training for future image consultants, and forming alliances with consultants who offer related services. This is par for the course for all self-employed stylists and consultants. She has had her own business for seven years and says it takes three to five years to get a corporate consulting business established.

EARNINGS

Earnings for personal stylists and image consultants are determined by the number of hours the individual works, the type of clientele, and the individual's location. Susan Fignar estimates that earnings start at under $20,000 but can reach $75,000 or more for top performers. Since many personal stylists and image consultants own their own businesses, it may also be helpful to consider that some small-business owners may earn only about $15,000 a year, while the most successful may make $100,000 or more.

Because most consultants are self-employed, they must provide their own insurance and other benefits.

WORK ENVIRONMENT

Many stylists and consultants are employed in corporate settings. Susan Fignar works at corporate sites and training facilities, speaks before various organizations, and has appeared on radio and television. She has contact with management and with human resources and training departments. Her work schedule has busy and slow periods, but she usually works from 40 to 50 hours a week and sometimes makes evening presentations. She describes her work as exciting, draining, and full of time constraints.

OUTLOOK

Employment for personal appearance workers is expected to grow as fast as the average for all occupations through 2014, according to the *Occupational Outlook Handbook,* mainly due to increasing population, incomes, and demand for cosmetology services.

Susan Fignar says corporate consultants are affected by downsizing because when companies cut personnel they also reduce training. "Right now," she says, "the field is growing." She says the hot topics are casual dress for business, etiquette, communications, and public image. Fignar feels security comes from constantly working to build one's consulting business. She advises consultants to develop a 60-second sales pitch so they're always ready to describe their services to any prospective client they meet.

FOR MORE INFORMATION

This organization has information on continuing education, mentorship programs, and certification.

Association of Image Consultants International
100 East Grand Avenue, Suite 330
Des Moines, IA 50309-1835
Tel: 515-282-5500
Email: info@aici.org
http://www.aici.org

Photographers, Publicity

OVERVIEW

Photographers take and sometimes develop and print pictures of people, places, objects, and events, using a variety of cameras and photographic equipment. They work in the publishing, advertising, public relations, science, and business industries, as well as provide personal photographic services. They may also work as fine artists or cinematographers. There are approximately 129,000 photographers employed in the United States.

HISTORY

The word *photograph* means "to write with light." Although the art of photography goes back only about 150 years, the two Greek words that were chosen and combined to refer to this skill quite accurately describe what it does.

The discoveries that led eventually to photography began early in the 18th century when a German scientist, Dr. Johann H. Schultze, experimented with the action of light on certain chemicals. He found that when these chemicals were covered by dark paper they did not change color, but when they were exposed to sunlight, they darkened. A French painter named Louis Daguerre became the first photographer in 1839, using silver-iodide-coated plates and a small box. To develop images on the plates, Daguerre exposed them to mercury vapor. The daguerreotype, as these early photographs came to be known, took minutes to expose and the developing process was directly to the plate. There were no prints made.

Although the daguerreotype was the sensation of its day, it was not until George Eastman invented a simple camera and flexible roll

QUICK FACTS

School Subjects
Art
Chemistry

Personal Skills
Artistic
Communication/ideas

Work Environment
Indoors and outdoors
Primarily multiple locations

Minimum Education Level
Some postsecondary training

Salary Range
$15,240 to $26,100 to $53,900+

Certification or Licensing
None available

Outlook
About as fast as the average

DOT
143

GOE
01.02.03

NOC
5221

O*NET-SOC
27-4021.01

film that photography began to come into widespread use in the late 1800s. After exposing this film to light and developing it with chemicals, the film revealed a color-reversed image, which is called a negative. To make the negative positive (aka: print a picture), light must be shone though the negative onto light-sensitive paper. This process can be repeated to make multiple copies of an image from one negative.

One of the most important developments in recent years is digital photography. In digital photography, instead of using film, pictures are recorded on microchips, which can then be downloaded onto a computer's hard drive. They can be manipulated in size, color, and shape, virtually eliminating the need for a darkroom.

New methods (such as digital photography) and new creative mediums (such as the Internet) have created many new opportunities for photographers, including those employed by public relations firms, corporations, nonprofit organizations, and government agencies.

THE JOB

Many photographers rely on public relations work or corporate photography for a large bulk of their assignments. They are often hired by the public relations department of a corporation to take formal portraits of executives or shoot photos to accompany a press release or for use on a Web site or in brochures. Photographers are often hired to document special events such as the opening of a new facility, a community event, or a corporate-sponsored charitable event. Some photographers may be asked to film an event for use in a video or Internet release.

Photography is both an artistic and technical occupation. There are many variables in the process that a knowledgeable photographer can manipulate to produce a clear image or a more abstract work of fine art. First, photographers know how to use cameras and can adjust focus, shutter speeds, aperture, lenses, and filters. They know about the types and speeds of films. Photographers also know about light and shadow, deciding when to use available natural light and when to set up artificial lighting to achieve desired effects.

Some photographers who work with still photography send their film to laboratories, but some develop their own negatives and make their own prints. These processes require knowledge of chemicals such as developers and fixers and how to use enlarging equipment. Photographers must also be familiar with the large variety of papers available for printing photographs, all of which deliver a different effect. Most photographers continually experiment with photographic processes to improve their technical proficiency or to create special effects.

Top U.S. Public Relations Firms by Revenue, 2005

Firm	Revenue (in millions)	Location	Web Site
1. Edelman	$170.8	Chicago	http://www.edelman.com
2. Waggener Edstrom	$79.1	Bellevue, Washington	http://www.waggenerstrom.com
3. The Ruder Finn Group	$74.4	New York	http://www.ruderfinn.com
4. APCO Worldwide	$41.8	Washington, D.C.	http://www.apcoworldwide.com
5. MWW Group	$41.0	East Rutherford, New Jersey	http://www.mww.com
6. Text 100 Public Relations	$25.3	San Francisco	http://www.text100.com
7. Chandler Chicco Agency	$25.2	New York	http://www.ccapr.com
8. Schwartz Communications	$22.1	Waltham, Massachusetts	http://www.schwartz-pr.com
9. PCGCampbell	$20.9	Dearborn, Michigan	http://www.pcgcampbell.com
10. Zeno Group	$19.6	New York	http://www.zenogroup.com

Source: *PRWeek*

Digital photography is a relatively new development. With this new technology, film is replaced by microchips that record pictures in digital format. Pictures can then be downloaded onto a computer's hard drive. Using special software, photographers can manipulate the images on the screen and place them directly onto the layout of a Web site or brochure. Many times, photographers work with public relations professionals such as designers and writers to create publicity campaigns.

Some photographers write for trade and technical journals, teach photography in schools and colleges, act as representatives of photographic equipment manufacturers, sell photographic equipment and supplies, produce documentary films, or do freelance work.

REQUIREMENTS

High School

While in high school, take as many art classes and photography classes that are available. Chemistry is useful for understanding developing and printing processes. You can learn about photo manipulation software and digital photography in computer classes, and business classes will help if you are considering a freelance career.

Postsecondary Training

A college education is not required to become a photographer, although college training probably offers the most promising assurance of success if you decide to pursue a career in fields such as industrial, news, or scientific photography. There are degree programs at the associate's, bachelor's, and master's levels. Many, however, become photographers with no formal education beyond high school.

To become a photographer, you should have a broad technical understanding of photography plus as much practical experience with cameras as possible. Take many different kinds of photographs with a variety of cameras and subjects. Learn how to develop photographs and, if possible, build your own darkroom or rent one. Experience in picture composition, cropping prints (cutting images to a desired size), enlarging, and retouching are all valuable.

Other Requirements

You should possess manual dexterity, good eyesight and color vision, and artistic ability to succeed in this line of work. You need an eye for form and line, an appreciation of light and shadow, and the ability to use imaginative and creative approaches to photographs or film, especially in commercial work. In addition, you should be patient and accurate and enjoy working with detail.

Self-employed (or freelance) photographers need good business skills. They must be able to manage their own studios, including hiring and managing assistants and other employees, keeping records, and maintaining photographic and business files. Marketing and sales skills are also important to a successful freelance photography business.

EXPLORING

Photography is a field that anyone with a camera can explore. To learn more about this career, you can join high school camera clubs, yearbook or newspaper staffs, photography contests, and community hobby groups. You can also seek a part-time or summer job in a camera shop or work as a developer in a laboratory or processing center.

If you are interested in becoming a publicity photographer, volunteer to take photographs for community and nonprofit organizations in your area. This will you give a good introduction to the field, and even allow you the chance to have your work published in press releases and at an organization's Web site.

EMPLOYERS

About 129,000 photographers work in the United States, more than half of whom are self-employed. Most jobs for photographers are provided by photographic or commercial art studios; other employers include public relations and advertising firms, newspapers and magazines, radio and TV broadcasting, film companies, government agencies, and manufacturing firms. Colleges, universities, and other educational institutions employ photographers to prepare promotional and educational materials.

STARTING OUT

Some photographers enter the field as apprentices, trainees, or assistants. Trainees may work in a darkroom, camera shop, or developing laboratory. They may move lights and arrange backgrounds for a publicity photographer. Assistants spend many months learning this kind of work before they move into a job behind a camera.

Many large cities offer schools of photography, which may be a good way to start in the field. Beginning photographers may work for a public relations firm, newspapers, or magazine in their area. Other photographers choose to go into business for themselves as soon as they have finished their formal education. Setting up a studio may not require a large capital outlay, but beginners may find that success does not come easily.

ADVANCEMENT

Because photography is such a diversified field, there is no usual way in which to get ahead. Those who begin by working for someone else may advance to owning their own businesses. Commercial photographers may gain prestige as more of their pictures are placed in well-known trade journals or popular magazines. A few photographers may become celebrities in their own right by making contributions to the art world or the sciences.

EARNINGS

The U.S. Department of Labor reports that salaried photographers had median annual earnings of $26,100 in 2005. Salaries ranged from less than $15,240 to more than $53,900. Photographers earned the following mean annual salaries in 2005 by industry: newspaper, book, and directory publishers, $37,230; radio and television broadcasting, $36,100; and colleges and universities, $38,590.

Self-employed photographers often earn more than salaried photographers, but their earnings depend on general business conditions. In addition, self-employed photographers do not receive the benefits that a company provides its employees.

Photographers in salaried jobs usually receive benefits such as paid holidays, vacations, and sick leave and medical insurance.

WORK ENVIRONMENT

Work conditions vary based on the job and employer. Many publicity photographers work a 35- to 40-hour workweek, but may have to work at night and on weekends when outreach programs, award dinners, and other events are held. Freelancers often work longer, more irregular hours.

In general, photographers work under pressure to meet deadlines and satisfy customers. Freelance photographers have the added pressure of uncertain incomes and have to continually seek out new clients.

For freelance photographers, the cost of equipment can be quite expensive, with no assurance that the money spent will be repaid through income from future assignments. For all photographers, flexibility is a major asset.

OUTLOOK

Employment of photographers will increase about as fast as the average for all occupations through 2014, according to the *Occupational Outlook Handbook*. The demand for new images should remain strong in education, communication, entertainment, marketing, and research. As the Internet grows and more companies and organizations turn to electronic publishing, demand will increase for photographers to produce digital images.

Photography is a highly competitive field. There are far more photographers than positions available. Only those who are extremely talented and highly skilled can support themselves as self-employed photographers. Many photographers take pictures as a sideline while working another job.

FOR MORE INFORMATION

The ASMP promotes the rights of photographers, educates its members in business practices, and promotes high standards of ethics.
American Society of Media Photographers (ASMP)
150 North Second Street
Philadelphia, PA 19106-1912
Tel: 215-451-2767
http://www.asmp.org

This organization provides training, publishes its own magazine, and offers various services for its members.
Professional Photographers of America
229 Peachtree Street, NE, Suite 2200
Atlanta, GA 30303-1608
Tel: 800-786-6277
Email: csc@ppa.com
http://www.ppa.com

For information on student membership, contact
Student Photographic Society
229 Peachtree Street, NE, Suite 2200
Atlanta, GA 30303-1608
Tel: 866-886-5325
Email: info@studentphoto.com
http://www.studentphoto.com

Political Speechwriters

QUICK FACTS

School Subjects
English
Government
Speech

Personal Skills
Communication/ideas
Following instructions

Work Environment
Primarily indoors
One location with some travel

Minimum Education Level
Bachelor's degree

Salary Range
$20,000 to $60,500 to $100,000+

Certification or Licensing
None available

Outlook
Little change

DOT
131

GOE
01.02.01

NOC
5121

O*NET-SOC
27-3043.00

OVERVIEW

Political speechwriters prepare speeches for individuals in the political arena. They write for politicians in all branches of government, from the local and state level to the national level, including the president of the United States.

HISTORY

History is filled with politicians who were renowned as great orators. But what about those who helped them write the compelling and memorable speeches? Undoubtedly, all politicians have had some help with writing their speeches through history. The first president of the United States, George Washington, is said to have received help with his speeches from Alexander Hamilton, the first secretary of the U.S. Department of the Treasury. A gentleman by the name of Judson Welliver is generally considered to be the first person employed as a speechwriter for a U.S. president, serving Calvin Coolidge in the 1920s. Nowadays, full-time speechwriters employed in the official White House Office of Speechwriting help the president craft memorable speeches. Presidents are not the only ones who sometimes need help creating a captivating and inspiring speech—politicians at every level and branch of government use speechwriters to communicate their ideas to a variety of audiences.

THE JOB

Political speechwriters write speeches for politicians, or they may assist the politician in composing a speech. A politician may need speechwriters for several reasons. Many politicians are extremely busy and simply do not have the time to write the many speeches they need to give. Others may not feel comfortable writing their own speeches and require the presence of a speechwriter to help them make sense of what they want to say, and how they want to convey that message in a speech. Still other politicians may have excellent ideas for their speeches but need help communicating their vision to others.

A political speechwriter usually begins writing a speech once a topic is selected. They may have a topic assigned to them, or they may have to determine the topic of the speech themselves. To do this, a speechwriter may meet with the politician they are writing for to receive his or her input. A speechwriter might also meet with representatives of the group the politician will be speaking to, in order to discover their concerns and ensure that they are addressed in the speech. Next, speechwriters will typically research the topic to be mentioned in the speech. To do this, they may use the resources of libraries, the Internet, or interview knowledgeable authorities in the field.

Once a speechwriter has gathered enough initial information, he or she begins to write the speech. Speechwriters must keep several things in mind while writing the speech. They need to make sure the speech sounds like it was written by the politician who will ultimately be delivering it. They also need to keep in mind who will be hearing the speech, making sure that the speech is written in a way that it will be not only understood by the intended audience, but that it will also prove to be persuasive and effective in delivering the politician's message. The speechwriter is also concerned with the mechanics of good speechwriting: allowing the speaker to engage the audience; providing clear, key points of the speech that can be easily recognized and digested by the audience; and making sure the audience identifies positively with the speaker by the end of the speech. They also have to be concerned with more mundane issues, such as making sure the speech does not exceed any time limits.

After the speechwriter finishes a rough draft of a speech, it will need to be approved by the politician delivering it. Depending on the individual, he or she may or may not have had any interaction with the speechwriter until this stage. The politician, as well as his or her advisers, may revise the speech and send it back to the speechwriter for additional work, changing anything the politician or advisers are not satisfied or comfortable with. At this point, the speech may be shuffled back and forth several more times before it is finally approved.

After the speech is approved, the speechwriter may be responsible for producing the speech in its final form, which varies across different situations. The speech may need to be typed on easily readable note cards for a politician speaking in a small auditorium, or the speech might need to be on a computer disk that can be input into a TelePrompTer and displayed on a monitor for the politician to read at a large rally or televised event.

REQUIREMENTS

High School

Since speechwriters need to be strong communicators, you should take as many English, speech, and communications courses as you can. Take courses in civics, history, and government as well. If possible, join a speech or debate team to gain experience researching current events, analyzing data, and presenting information to others.

Postsecondary Training

You will need a bachelor's degree, preferably in a field related to communications or political science, to become a political speechwriter. In addition to taking as many writing, speech, and communications classes as you can, you should pursue a well-rounded education, taking courses in history and politics.

Other Requirements

To be a successful speechwriter, you must stay up-to-date with current events and daily news. You must be flexible and able to integrate late-breaking news items into speeches you have written. You must also be able to work under pressure and meet deadlines. Because speechwriters need to interact with others, you should have good people skills.

EXPLORING

The best way to find out if speechwriting is something you wish to pursue is to write—anything—as often as possible. The more you write, the more you will improve your skills. You can practice writing speeches on your own, or you can participate with your school's speech or debate teams. Join local groups to learn the basics of effective public speaking so you can write more successful speeches. Reading famous speeches will also help you to understand the components of a successful speech. You can also join nonprofit or political organizations and offer to assist with public speaking events.

This will give you the opportunity to make contacts, observe their operations, and you might even get an opportunity to assist a speechwriter with research.

EMPLOYERS

Most political speechwriters work for politicians or political consulting groups. Many jobs are in Washington, D.C., but there are opportunities available across the nation at the state and local government levels. One thing to keep in mind: It can be very difficult to write speeches supporting issues that go against you own views or morals. If you find employment with a politician who is closely aligned with your own opinions on issues that are important to you, your job will be easier and have the potential to be very rewarding.

STARTING OUT

One of the most important and effective ways of getting started as a political speechwriter is to make connections with people involved in politics. Volunteer for political campaigns and be an advocate of public policy issues that interest you. You can make good connections, and gain valuable experience, working or interning in the offices of your state capital. You might also try for an internship with one of your state's members of Congress; contact their offices in Washington, D.C., for internship applications.

Some people pursue a career as a political speechwriter directly by working in the press offices of political candidates, starting out as assistants to speechwriters or press secretaries, advancing as they are able to demonstrate their ability and as opportunities arise. Others make the jump to speechwriting after having worked in the political arena as lawyers, lobbyists, or journalists.

ADVANCEMENT

Political speechwriters have many advancement options. Entry-level speechwriters may progress from doing mostly research, to writing some low-profile speeches, to writing more important speeches. They may also start by working with politicians at the local level and move on to work with more prestigious politicians at the state or national levels. Or they may find themselves promoted to speechwriting positions that have more supervisory and organizational responsibilities, such as managing a team of speechwriters.

Some political speechwriters advance to non-speechwriting positions within public administration; for example, they may become politicians or political consultants. They may also make the transition to a career in media, finding employment as a writer, journalist, or a career in public relations.

EARNINGS

Salaries for speechwriters (including political speechwriters) range from $53,000 to $68,000, with a median salary of $60,500. Entry-level speechwriters typically earn much less, sometimes starting around $20,000, and experienced speechwriters who work with high-profile politicians may make considerably more, earning salaries of $100,000 or more. Salaries also depend on geographical location and the level of government for which the speechwriter writes.

WORK ENVIRONMENT

The work environment of political speechwriters can vary. At times, they may find themselves working in a relatively quiet office. They may also find themselves traveling on a crowded bus, train, or plane with the politician for whom they are writing, trying to craft a speech that needs to be finished by the time they arrive at their next destination. Work hours in this profession can be long and very irregular. This is especially the case when a speechwriter is working for a major political candidate on the campaign trail.

The work environment, whether it is on the road or in the office, has the potential to be frantic, noisy, and stressful. Politicians, political advisers, and speechwriters may have opposing views of what needs to be included in a speech, leading to heated exchanges. Speechwriters may have to make last-minute changes to a speech based on the day's news events, all with the stress of deadlines looming. That said, not all speechwriters are employed in these high-pressured settings. Depending on their employer, a speechwriter may also work in a typical office environment, with fairly regular work hours.

OUTLOOK

The U.S. Department of Labor does not provide employment outlook information for the career of political speechwriter. It is safe to say, though, given the prevalence of politics and the importance of effective communication in the world today, that political speechwriters will have steady employment opportunities for the next decade.

FOR MORE INFORMATION

This organization provides professional guidance, assistance, and education to members and maintains a code of ethics.
American Association of Political Consultants
600 Pennsylvania Avenue, SE, Suite 330
Washington, DC 20003-6300
Tel: 202-544-9815
Email: info@theaapc.org
http://www.theaapc.org

Visit the Web sites of the House and the Senate for press releases and links to sites for individual members of Congress to inquire about internship opportunities. To write to your state's representatives, contact
Office of Congressperson (Name)
U.S. House of Representatives
Washington, DC 20515
http://www.house.gov

Office of Senator (Name)
United States Senate
Washington, DC 20510
http://www.senate.gov

To gain insight into effective public speaking, contact
Toastmasters International
23182 Arroyo Vista
Rancho Santa Margarita, CA 92688-2699
Tel: 949-858-8255
http://www.toastmasters.org

Press Secretaries and Political Consultants

OVERVIEW

Press secretaries, political consultants, and other media relations professionals help politicians promote themselves and their issues among voters. They advise politicians on how to address the media. Sometimes called *spin doctors*, these professionals use the media to either change or strengthen public opinion. Press secretaries work for candidates and elected officials, while political consultants work with firms, contracting their services to politicians. The majority of press secretaries and political consultants work in Washington, D.C.; others work all across the country, involved with local and state government officials and candidates.

HISTORY

Using the media for political purposes is nearly as old as the U.S. government itself. The news media developed right alongside the political parties, and early newspapers served as a battleground for the Federalists and the Republicans. The first media moguls of the late 1800s often saw their newspapers as podiums from which to promote themselves. George Hearst bought the *San Francisco Examiner* in 1885 for the sole purpose of helping him campaign for Congress.

The latter half of the 20th century introduced whole other forms of media, which were quickly exploited by politicians seeking offices. Many historians mark the Kennedy-Nixon debate of 1960 as the moment when television coverage first became a key factor in the election process. Those who read of the debate in the next day's

QUICK FACTS

School Subjects
English
Government
Journalism

Personal Skills
Communication/ideas
Leadership/management

Work Environment
Primarily indoors
One location with some
    travel

Minimum Education Level
Bachelor's degree

Salary Range
$26,870 to $45,020 to
    $116,573+

Certification or Licensing
None available

Outlook
About as fast as the average

DOT
N/A

GOE
N/A

NOC
N/A

O*NET-SOC
N/A

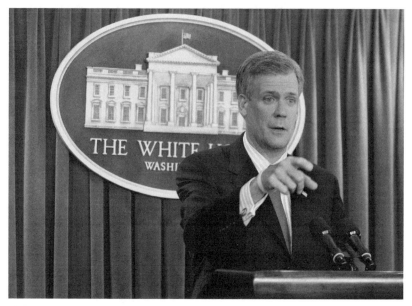

White House press secretary Tony Snow takes a question from a member of the press. *(Corbis)*

newspapers were under the impression that Nixon had easily won, but it was Kennedy's composure and appeal on camera that made the most powerful impression. Negative campaigning first showed its powerful influence in 1964, when Democratic presidential candidate Lyndon Johnson ran ads featuring a girl picking a flower while a nuclear bomb exploded in the background, which commented on Republican candidate Barry Goldwater's advocacy of strong military action in Vietnam.

Bill Clinton was probably the first president to benefit from the art of spin, as his press secretaries and political managers were actively involved in dealing with his scandals and keeping his approval ratings high among the public. James Carville and George Stephanopoulos, working for Clinton's 1992 campaign, had the task of playing up Clinton's strengths as an intelligent, gifted politician, while downplaying his questionable moral background. Their efforts were portrayed in the documentary *The War Room*, and their success earned them national renown as spin doctors.

THE JOB

If you were to manage a political campaign, how would you go about publicizing the candidate to the largest number of voters? You'd use television, of course. The need for TV and radio spots during a campaign is the reason it costs so much today to run for office. And it's also the reason many politicians hire professionals with an understanding of media relations to help them get elected. Once elected, a politician continues to rely on media relations experts, such as press secretaries, political consultants, and political managers, to use the media to portray the politician in the best light. In recent years, such words as *spin*, *leak*, and *sound bite* have entered the daily vocabulary of news and politics to describe elements of political coverage in the media.

Political consultants usually work independently, or as members of consulting firms, and contract with individuals. Political consultants are involved in producing radio and TV ads, writing campaign plans, and developing themes for these campaigns. A theme may focus on a specific issue or on the differences between the client and the opponent. Their client may be new to the political arena or someone established looking to maintain an office. They conduct polls and surveys to gauge public opinion and to identify their client's biggest competition. Political consultants advise their clients in the best ways to use the media. In addition to TV and radio, the Internet has proven important to politicians. Consultants launch campaign Web sites and also chase down rumors that spread across the Internet. A consultant may be hired for an entire campaign, or may be hired only to produce an ad, or to come up with a sound bite (or catchy quote) for the media.

Though voters across the country complain about negative campaigning, or mudslinging, such campaigns have proven effective. In his 1988 presidential campaign, George H. W. Bush ran TV ads featuring the now notorious Willie Horton, a convict who was released from prison only to commit another crime. The ad was intended to draw attention to what Bush considered his opponent's soft approach to crime. It proved very effective in undermining the campaign of Michael Dukakis and putting him on the defensive. Many consultants believe they must focus on a few specific issues in a campaign, emphasizing their client's strengths as well as the opponent's weaknesses.

Press secretaries serve on the congressional staffs of senators and representatives and on the staffs of governors and mayors. The president also has a press secretary. Press secretaries and their assistants write press releases and opinion pieces to publicize the efforts of the government officials for whom they work. They also help prepare speeches and prepare their employers for press conferences and interviews. They maintain Web sites, posting press releases and the results of press conferences.

Media relations experts are often called *spin doctors* because of their ability to manipulate the media, or put a good spin on a news story to best suit the purposes of their clients. Corporations also rely on spin for positive media coverage. Media relations experts are often called upon during a political scandal, or after corporate blunders, for damage control. Using the newspapers and radio and TV broadcasts, spin doctors attempt to downplay public relations disasters, helping politicians and corporations save face. In highly sensitive situations, they must answer questions selectively and carefully, and they may even be involved in secretly releasing, or leaking, information to the press. Because of these manipulations, media relations professionals are often disrespected. They're sometimes viewed as people who conceal facts and present lies, prey on the emotions of voters, or even represent companies responsible for illegal practices. However, many political consultants and media representatives are responsible for bringing public attention to important issues and good political candidates. They also help organizations and nonprofit groups advocate for legislative issues and help develop support for school funding, environmental concerns, and other community needs.

REQUIREMENTS

High School

English composition, drama, and speech classes will help you develop good communication skills, while government, history, and civics classes will teach you about the structure of local, state, and federal government. Take math, economics, and accounting courses to prepare for poll-taking and for analyzing statistics and demographics.

While in high school, work with your school newspaper, radio station, or TV station. This will help you recognize how important reporters, editors, and producers are in putting together newspapers and shaping news segments. You should also consider joining your school's speech and debate team to gain experience in research and in persuasive argument.

Postsecondary Training

Most people in media relations have bachelor's degrees, and some also hold master's degrees, doctorates, and law degrees. As an undergraduate, you should enroll in a four-year college and pursue a well-rounded education. Press secretaries and political consultants need a good understanding of the history and culture of the United States and foreign countries. Some of the majors you should consider as an undergraduate are journalism, political science, English, marketing, and economics. You should take courses in government, psychology, statistics, history of western civilization, and a foreign language. You might then choose to pursue a graduate degree in journalism, political science, public administration, or international relations.

Seek a college with a good internship program. You might also pursue internships with local and state officials and your congressional members in the Senate and House of Representatives. Journalism internships will involve you with local and national publications, or the news departments of radio and TV stations.

Other Requirements

In this career, you need to be very organized and capable of juggling many different tasks, from quickly writing ads and press releases to developing budgets and expense accounts. You need good problem-solving skills and some imagination when putting a positive spin on negative issues. Good people skills are important so that you can develop contacts within government and the media. You should feel comfortable with public speaking, leading press conferences, and speaking on behalf of your employers and clients. You should also enjoy competition. You can't be intimidated by people in power or by journalists questioning the issues addressed in your campaigns.

EXPLORING

Get involved with your school government as well as with committees and clubs that have officers and elections. You can also become involved in local, state, and federal elections by volunteering for campaigns; though you may just be making phone calls and putting up signs, you may also have the opportunity to write press releases and schedule press conferences and interviews, and you will see first-hand how a campaign operates.

Working for your school newspaper will help you learn about conducting research, interviews, and opinion polls, which all play a part in managing media relations. You may be able to get a part-time job or an internship with your city's newspaper or broadcast news station, where you will gain experience with election coverage and political advertising. Visit the Web sites of U.S. Congress members. Many sites feature lists of recent press releases, which will give you a sense of how a press office publicizes the efforts and actions of Congress members. Read some of the many books examining recent political campaigns and scandals, and read magazines like *Harper's* (http://www.harpers.org), *The Atlantic* (http://www.theatlantic.com), and the online magazine *Salon.com* (http://www.salonmag.com) for political commentary.

EMPLOYERS

Though a majority of press secretaries and political consultants work in Washington, D.C., others work in state capitals and major cities all across the country. Press secretaries work for local, state, and federal government officials. They also find work with public relations agencies, and the press offices of large corporations. Celebrities, and others in the public eye also hire press agents to help them control rumors and publicity.

Political consultants are generally self-employed, or work for consulting firms that specialize in media relations. They contract with politicians, corporations, nonprofit groups, and trade and professional associations. They participate in the campaigns of mayors, governors, and Congress members as well as in the political campaigns of other countries.

STARTING OUT

Media relations jobs are not advertised, and there is no predetermined path to success. It is recommended that you make connections with people in both politics and the media. Volunteer for political campaigns, and also advocate for public policy issues of interest to you. You can make good connections, and gain valuable experience, working or interning in the offices of your state capital. You might also try for an internship with one of your state's members of Congress; contact their offices in Washington, D.C., for internship applications. If you are more interested in the writing and producing aspects of the career, work for local newspapers or the broadcast news media; or work as a producer for a television production crew or for an ad agency that specializes in political campaigns. A political consulting firm may hire assistants for writing and for commercial production. Whereas some people pursue the career directly by working in the press offices of political candidates, others find their way into political consulting after having worked as lawyers, lobbyists, or journalists.

ADVANCEMENT

A press secretary who has worked closely with a successful government official may advance into a higher staff position, like chief of staff or legislative director. Political consultants, after winning many elections and establishing credentials, will begin to take on more prominent clients and major campaigns. Network TV, cable, and radio news departments also hire successful media relations experts to serve as political analysts on the air. Some consultants also write columns for newspapers and syndicates and publish books about their insights into politics.

EARNINGS

According to the U.S. Department of Labor, public relations specialists (which includes press secretaries) had median annual earnings of $45,020 in 2005, with salaries ranging from less than $26,870 to more than $84,300. In 2005, mean earnings for those who worked in local government were $48,460, and for those in federal government, $72,600.

According to the Congressional Management Foundation (CMF), a consulting firm in Washington, D.C., press secretaries working in the U.S. House of Representatives earned less than their counterparts in the Senate. The CMF found that the average pay of a House press secretary was $45,301, while those employed by the Senate earned an average of $116,573. This pay differential is probably even greater, because the CMF info for the Senate is from 1999, while the House data is from 2000.

The incomes of political consultants vary greatly. Someone contracting with local candidates, or with state organizations and associations, may make around $40,000 a year; someone consulting with high-profile candidates may earn hundreds of thousands of dollars a year.

WORK ENVIRONMENT

Representing politicians can be thankless work. Press secretaries may have to speak to the press about sensitive, volatile issues and deal directly with the frustrations of journalists unable to get the answers they want. When working for prominent politicians, they may become the subject of personal attacks.

Despite these potential conflicts, the work can be exciting and fast-paced. Press secretaries and political consultants see the results of their efforts in the newspapers and on television, and they have the satisfaction of influencing voters and public opinion. If working on a campaign as a consultant, their hours will be long and stressful. In some cases, they'll have to scrap unproductive media ads and start from scratch with only hours to write, produce, and place new commercials. They'll also have to be available to their clients around the clock.

OUTLOOK

Employment for press secretaries and political consultants is expected to grow about as fast as the average. Consultants and media representatives will become increasingly important to candidates and elected officials. Television ads and Internet campaigns have become almost necessary to reach the public. The work of press secretaries will expand as more news networks and news magazines closely follow the decisions and actions of government officials.

The Pew Research Center, which surveys public opinion on political issues, has found that most Americans are concerned about negative campaigning, while most political consultants see nothing wrong with using negative tactics in advertising. Despite how the general public may feel about negative campaigning, it remains a very effective tool for consultants. In some local elections, candidates may mutually agree to avoid the mudslinging, but the use of negative ads in general is likely to increase.

This negative campaigning may be affected somewhat by developing technology. Voters are now able to access more information about candidates and issues via the Internet. Also, the increase in the number of channels available to cable TV viewers makes it more difficult for candidates to advertise to a general audience. However, the greater number of outlets for media products will create an increased demand for writers, TV producers, and Web designers to help candidates reach potential voters.

FOR MORE INFORMATION

This organization provides professional guidance, assistance, and education to members and maintains a code of ethics.
American Association of Political Consultants
600 Pennsylvania Avenue, SE, Suite 330
Washington, DC 20003-6300
Tel: 202-544-9815
Email: info@theaapc.org
http://www.theaapc.org

For general information about careers in broadcast media, contact
National Association of Broadcasters
1771 N Street, NW
Washington, DC 20036-2800

Tel: 202-429-5300
Email: nab@nab.org
http://www.nab.org

Visit the Web sites of the House and the Senate for press releases and links to sites for individual members of Congress. To write to your state representatives, contact
Office of Congressperson (Name)
U.S. House of Representatives
Washington, DC 20515
http://www.house.gov

Office of Senator (Name)
United States Senate
Washington, DC 20510
http://www.senate.gov

The Pew Research Center is an opinion research group that studies attitudes toward press, politics, and public policy issues. To read some of their survey results, visit its Web site or contact
The Pew Research Center for the People and the Press
1615 L Street, NW, Suite 700
Washington, DC 20036-5621
Tel: 202-419-4350
Email: info@people-press.org
http://www.people-press.org

Public Opinion Researchers

OVERVIEW

Public opinion researchers help measure public sentiment about various products, services, or social issues by gathering information from a sample of the population through questionnaires and interviews. They collect, analyze, and interpret data and opinions to explore issues and forecast trends. Their poll results help business people, politicians, and other decision makers determine what's on the public's mind. It is estimated that there are fewer than 100,000 full-time employees currently in the field, primarily working for the government or private industry in large cities.

HISTORY

Public opinion research began in a rudimentary way in the 1830s and 1840s when local newspapers asked their readers to fill out unofficial ballots indicating for whom they had voted in a particular election. Since that time, research on political issues has been conducted with increasing frequency—especially during presidential election years. However, public opinion research is most widely used by businesses to determine what products or services consumers like or dislike.

As questionnaires and interviewing techniques have become more refined, the field of public opinion research has become more accurate at reflecting the individual attitudes and opinions of the sample groups. Companies like The Gallup Organization and Harris Interactive conduct surveys for a wide range of political and economic purposes. Although some people continue to question the accuracy

QUICK FACTS

School Subjects
Business
Mathematics
Psychology

Personal Skills
Communication/ideas
Technical/scientific

Work Environment
Indoors and outdoors
Primarily multiple locations

Minimum Education Level
Bachelor's degree

Salary Range
$16,080 to $57,300 to $108,990+

Certification or Licensing
None available

Outlook
Faster than the average

DOT
205

GOE
07.04.01

NOC
1454

O*NET-SOC
19-3021.00, 19-3022.00

A public opinion researcher records survey responses from an attendee at a design and remodeling show. (The Image Works)

and importance of polls, they have become an integral part of our social fabric.

THE JOB

Public opinion researchers conduct interviews and gather data that accurately reflect public opinions. They do this so decision makers in the business and political worlds have a better idea of what people want on a wide range of issues. Public opinion is sometimes gauged by interviewing a small percentage of the population containing a variety of people who closely parallel the larger population in terms of age, race, income, and other factors. At other times, researchers interview people who represent a certain demographic group. Public opinion researchers may help a company implement a new marketing strategy or help a political candidate decide which campaign issues the public considers important.

Researchers use a variety of methods to collect and analyze public opinion. The particular method depends on the target audience and the type of information desired. For example, if the owner of a shopping mall is interested in gauging the opinions of shoppers, the research company will most likely station interviewers in selected areas around the mall so they can question the shoppers. On the other hand, a public relations firm may be interested in the opinions of a particular demographic group, such as working mothers or teenagers. In this case, the research firm would plan a procedure (such as a telephone survey) providing access to that group. Other field collection methods include interviews in the home and at work as well as questionnaires that are filled out by respondents and then returned through the mail.

Planning is an important ingredient in developing an effective survey method. After they receive an assignment, researchers decide what portion of the population they will survey and develop questions that will result in an accurate gauging of opinion. Researchers investigate whether previous surveys have been done on a particular topic, and if so, what the results were.

It is important that exactly the same procedures be used throughout the entire data collection process so that the survey is not influenced by the individual styles of the interviewers. For this reason, the process is closely monitored by supervisory personnel. *Research assistants* help train survey interviewers, prepare survey questionnaires and related materials, and tabulate and code survey results.

Other specialists within the field include *market research analysts,* who collect, analyze, and interpret survey results to determine what they mean. They prepare reports and make recommendations on subjects ranging from preferences of prospective customers to future sales trends. They use mathematical and statistical models to analyze research. Research analysts are careful to screen out unimportant or invalid information that could skew their survey results. Some research analysts specialize in one industry or area. For example, *agricultural marketing research analysts* prepare sales forecasts for food businesses, which use the information in their advertising and sales programs. *Survey workers* conduct public opinion interviews to determine people's buying habits or opinions on public issues. Survey workers contact people in their homes, at work, at random in public places, or via the telephone, questioning the person in a specified manner, usually following a questionnaire format.

At times public opinion researchers are mistaken for telemarketers. According to the Council for Marketing and Opinion Research, public opinion researchers are conducting serious research, collecting opinions whereas telemarketers ultimately are in the business of sales.

REQUIREMENTS

High School

Because the ability to communicate in both spoken and written form is crucial for this job, you should take courses in English, speech arts, and social studies while in high school. In addition, take mathematics (especially statistics) and any courses in journalism or psychology that are available. Knowledge of a foreign language is also helpful.

Postsecondary Training

A college degree in economics or business administration provides a good background for public opinion researchers. A degree in sociology or psychology will be helpful for those interested in studying consumer demand or opinion research, while work in statistics or engineering might be more useful for those interested in certain types of industrial or analytical research.

Because of the increasingly sophisticated techniques used in public opinion research, most employers expect researchers to be familiar with computer applications, and many require a master's degree in business administration, sociology, educational psychology, or political science. While a doctorate is not necessary for most researchers, it is highly desirable for those who plan to become involved with complex research studies or work in an academic environment.

Other Requirements

Public opinion researchers who conduct interviews must be outgoing and enjoy interacting with a wide variety of people. Because much of the work involves getting people to reveal their personal opinions and beliefs, you must be a good listener and as nonjudgmental as possible. You must be patient and be able to handle rejection because some people may be uncooperative during the interviewing process.

If you choose to work in data analysis, you should be able to pay close attention to detail and spend long hours analyzing complex data. You may experience some pressure when forced to collect data or solve a problem within a specified period of time. If you intend to plan questionnaires, you will need good analytical skills and a strong command of the English language.

EXPLORING

High school students can often work as survey workers for a telemarketing firm or other consumer research company. Work opportunities may also be available where you can learn about the coding and tabulation of survey data. Actual participation in a consumer survey may also offer insight into the type of work involved in the field. You should also try to talk with professionals already working in the field to learn more about the profession.

EMPLOYERS

Fewer than 100,000 full-time public opinion researchers are employed in the field. Public opinion workers are primarily employed by private companies, such as public and private research firms and advertising agencies. They also work for the government and for various colleges and universities, often in research and teaching capacities. As is usually the case, those with the most experience and education should find the greatest number of job opportunities. Gaining experience in a specific area (such as food products) can give prospective researchers an edge.

STARTING OUT

Many people enter the field in a support position such as a survey worker, and with experience become interviewers or work as data analysts. Those with applicable education, training, and experience may begin as interviewers or data analysts. College career services counselors can often help qualified students find an appropriate position in public opinion research. Contacts can also be made through summer employment or by locating public and private research companies in the phone book.

ADVANCEMENT

Advancement opportunities are numerous in the public opinion research field. Often a research assistant will be promoted to a position as an interviewer or data analyst and, after sufficient experience in these or other aspects of research project development, become involved in a supervisory or planning capacity.

With a master's degree or doctorate, a person can become a manager of a large private research organization or marketing research director for an industrial or business firm. Those with extended work experience in public opinion research and with sufficient credentials may choose to start their own companies. Opportunities also exist in university teaching or research and development.

EARNINGS

Starting salaries vary according to the skill and experience of the applicant, the nature of the position, and the size of the company. The U.S. Department of Labor (USDL) does not offer salary information for public opinion researchers. It does report that market research analysts (a type of public opinion researcher) earned a median salary of $57,300 in 2005. Earnings ranged from less than $31,530 to $108,990 or more. The department also reports that survey workers earned salaries in

2005 that ranged from less than $16,080 to more than $70,450. The median annual salary for survey workers was $31,140 in 2005. Those in academic positions may earn somewhat less than their counterparts in the business community, but federal government salaries are competitive with those in the private sector.

Most full-time public opinion researchers receive the usual medical, pension, vacation, and other benefits that other professional workers do. Managers may also receive bonuses based on their company's performance.

WORK ENVIRONMENT

Public opinion researchers usually work a standard 40-hour week, although they may have to work overtime occasionally if a project has a tight deadline. Those in supervisory positions may work especially long hours overseeing the collection and interpretation of information.

When conducting telephone interviews or organizing or analyzing data, researchers work in comfortable offices, with calculators, computers, and data processing equipment close at hand. When collecting information via personal interviews or questionnaires, it is not unusual to spend time outside in shopping malls, on the street, or in private homes. Some evening and weekend work may be involved because people are most readily available to be interviewed at those times. Some research positions may include assignments that involve travel, but these are generally short assignments.

OUTLOOK

According to the U.S. Department of Labor, employment of market and survey research workers is expected to grow faster than the average for all occupations through 2014. Job opportunities should be ample for those trained in public opinion research, particularly those with graduate degrees. Those who specialize in marketing, mathematics, and statistics will have the best opportunities. Marketing research firms, financial services organizations, health care institutions, advertising firms, public relations firms, and insurance firms are potential employers.

FOR MORE INFORMATION

For more information on market research, contact
Advertising Research Foundation
432 Park Avenue South

New York, NY 10016-8013
Tel: 212-751-5656
Email: info@thearf.org
http://www.thearf.org

For information on graduate programs, contact
American Association for Public Opinion Research
PO Box 14263
Lenexa, KS 66285-4263
Tel: 913-895-4601
Email: AAPOR-info@goAMP.com
http://www.aapor.org

For career development information, contact
American Marketing Association
311 South Wacker Drive, Suite 5800
Chicago, IL 60606-6629
Tel: 800-262-1150
http://www.marketingpower.com

For comprehensive information on market and opinion research,
contact
Council for Marketing and Opinion Research
110 National Drive, 2nd Floor
Glastonbury, CT 06033-1212
Tel: 860-657-1881
Email: information@cmor.org
http://www.cmor.org

For information on survey research and graduate programs,
contact
Council of American Survey Research Organizations
170 North Country Road, Suite 4
Port Jefferson, NY 11777-2606
Tel: 631-928-6954
Email: casro@casro.org
http://www.casro.org

For career information, contact
Marketing Research Association
110 National Drive, 2nd Floor
Glastonbury, CT 06033-1212
Tel: 860-682-1000
http://www.mra-net.org

The following companies are leaders in survey and marketing research.

The Gallup Organization
http://www.gallup.com

Harris Interactive
http://www.harrisinteractive.com

Public Relations Managers

OVERVIEW

Public relations managers are responsible for influencing the public's image and recognition of their client, be it a large corporation, a service, or an individual. This is done through a carefully set plan of public appearances, public relations campaigns, press releases, surveys, and other scheduled events. Public relations managers, especially at large corporations, oversee the work of many staff members such as public relations specialists, researchers, designers, and administrators. There are approximately 58,000 public relations managers employed in the United States.

HISTORY

The origins of public relations date back to the time of ancient Greece, when philosophers such as Socrates and Plato used their oratory skills to persuade the public to agree with their views.

One of the first public relations specialists was Ivy Ledbetter Lee, a newspaper reporter. He was hired by the Standard Oil Company, as well as the family of John D. Rockefeller Jr., to manage the company crisis brought on by unrest by coal miners. Another early industry pioneer was Edward Bernays, often referred to as the "father of public relations." He listed actors, presidents, the government, nonprofit organizations, and large corporations as clients. One of his most memorable and successful public relations campaigns was for Proctor & Gamble's Ivory Soap. Public surveys indicated the nation's preference for unscented

QUICK FACTS

School Subjects
Business
Computer science

Personal Skills
Helping/teaching
Leadership/management

Work Environment
Primarily indoors
Primarily one location

Minimum Education Level
Bachelor's degree

Salary Range
$40,870 to $76,450 to
$145,600+

Certification or Licensing
Voluntary

Outlook
Faster than the average

DOT
165

GOE
11.09.03

NOC
0611

O*NET-SOC
11-2031.00

A team of public relations managers discuss a new publicity campaign. *(Corbis)*

soap. He capitalized on the fact that Ivory Soap so happened to be the only unscented soap on the market. Bernays organized sporting events such as soap yacht races in New York's Central Park, and nationwide contests such as the annual Ivory soap sculpting contest, promoting the product to the public. All events were widely covered in the media.

Chester Burger, another pioneer, was one of the first public relations professionals to use the medium of television to tell a story. His clientele included Sears Roebuck, the American Cancer Society, and Texas Instruments Inc.

In 1947, the Public Relations Society of America was founded as a way to establish industry standards and provide support and education for public relations professionals. In the 1950s, it established the "Code for the Professional Standards for the Practice of Public Relations," which is still widely used by the industry.

THE JOB

Public relations managers may supervise a team of public relations specialists or an entire department. Specialists, designers, artists, copywriters, media relations specialists, administrative assistants, are just a few of the workers who report to the public relations manager. Public relations managers work in all types of industries. For example, health care companies such as Baxter Healthcare rely on public relations managers to lead teams that raise public awareness and interest in a drug that is currently being reviewed by the Food and Drug Administration. Public relations managers are indispensable to politicians during election times in bringing the candidate's views and message to the voters, while at the same time negatively defining their opponents. Those in the entertainment or sports industries also rely on public relations managers to develop public relations campaigns to raise their Q-rating—a person' measure of visibility and likeability—in hopes of also increasing their market potential.

When creating a publicity program, public relations managers first identify the target audience—the group of people specifically affected by the product, service, idea, or individual being promoted. Once the target audience is ascertained, the manager then assigns tasks—such as writing press releases and arranging personal appearances and interviews—to his or her staff. After the project is assigned, managers monitor their staff and the progress of the campaign to ensure that everything is going as planned. They rely heavily on research to do their jobs. They may tweak or revise a plan according to the results of public surveys, opinion polls, or demographic analyses. They may also alter a plan after consultation with company executives or input from their staff.

Supervision is an important part of the job. Public relations managers review new programs and publicity campaigns, and are responsible for their implementation and success. An unfavorable review or client dissatisfaction will ultimately be the manager's responsibility to rectify. Conducting staff performance reviews, maintaining databases, and determining departments' budgets are also part of the manager's job description.

Public relations managers may work with the advertising, marketing, or financial departments of their company to create newsletters, brochures, annual reports, or the content of the company's Web site. Company executives may confer with managers before giving interviews or addressing major stockholders. Public relations managers often act as the corporate spokesperson when giving interviews or responding to requests from the media for information about the company or its products or services.

REQUIREMENTS
High School
You can prepare for a career as a public relations manager by taking college preparatory classes. Concentrate on courses that will improve your communication skills, such as speech, English, and

creative writing. Also, you should aim to study business-related subjects such as marketing, economics, public relations, management, and computer science.

Postsecondary Training
Most public relations managers have a bachelor's or master's degree in public relations, communications, or journalism. Others have entered the industry with a business, fine arts, or liberal arts degree, though with some concentration in public relations, advertising, or communications. Useful college classes include psychology, sociology, business, economics, and any art medium. Graduate and professional degrees are common at the managerial level.

Certification and Licensing
Many candidates on the executive track find it very helpful to pursue certification in this field. The Public Relations Society of America and the International Association of Business Communicators accredit public relations workers who have at least five years of experience in the field and pass a comprehensive examination.

Other Requirements
Having excellent communication skills, the ability to work on multiple projects, and superior management skills are imperative to becoming a successful public relations manager. Managing an entire department, dealing with other business executives, or interacting with a difficult client are often daily tests for workers in this career. You must be able to work well under stressful situations and tight deadlines, be able to delegate responsibilities, and effectively communicate your ideas to various staff members.

Other traits considered important for public relations managers are intelligence, decisiveness, intuition, creativity, honesty, loyalty, a sense of responsibility, and planning abilities.

EXPLORING
You can explore this field by doing promotional work for a school club or participating in other activities that catch your interest. For example, you can write a press release about an upcoming fundraising activity sponsored by the student council and send it out to the local media. Have the school photography club take pictures of the event as well. Finally, send a report about the fund-raising project's success, along with photos or video footage, to the local newspaper, town news bulletin, district Web site, or local cable channel.

You can also explore this career by developing your managerial skills in general. Whether you're involved in drama, sports, school publications, or a part-time job, there are managerial duties associated with any organized activity. These can involve planning, scheduling, managing other workers or volunteers, fund-raising, or budgeting.

EMPLOYERS

Approximately 58,000 public relations managers are employed in the United States. While employment opportunities exist in every industry, jobs may be more plentiful with businesses that provide some type of service. Examples include health care—hospitals, clinics, medical equipment manufacturers; educational services—publishers or universities and colleges; professional, scientific, or technical services—financial institutions and planners, computer manufacturers, or laboratories. Public relations managers may need to relocate because many management-track jobs at desirable companies are located in larger, more urban areas.

STARTING OUT

You will first need experience in lower-level public relations jobs before advancing to a managerial position. As an assistant, your duties may include updating databases, assembling media kits, or helping with the many details of a fund-raising event. With more experience, you may be given more responsibilities or assigned more prestigious accounts and projects.

To break into a public relations firm, visit your college placement office for job leads. In addition, many firms advertise job listings in newspapers and on Internet job boards.

ADVANCEMENT

Promotion to director of public relations or other executive positions within a company are common advancement routes for managers. To stay competitive, you may want to continue your education, either with a master's degree in public relations or business administration.

Another advancement possibility includes moving to a company with a larger public relations budget and staff, and possibly higher compensation. Some experienced managers may opt to start their own public relations firm, or work as a public relations consultant on a freelance basis.

Top Employers of Public Relations Managers, 2005

Employer	# Employed	Mean Annual Earnings
Advertising and related services	3,690	$115,090
Management of companies and enterprises	3,460	$101,530
Colleges and universities	3,380	$77,790
Professional and similar organizations	3,140	$85,640
Local government	2,680	$65,500

Source: U.S. Department of Labor

Advancement may be accelerated by participating in advanced training programs sponsored by industry and trade associations or by enrolling in continued education programs at colleges and universities. Firms sometimes offer tuition reimbursement for these programs. Managers committed to improving their knowledge of the field and of related disciplines—especially computer information systems—will have the best opportunities for advancement.

EARNINGS

Public relations managers had median annual earnings of $76,450 in 2005, according to the U.S. Department of Labor. Salaries ranged from less than $40,870 to $145,600 or more annually. However, many factors may affect salary, such as the size and industry of a business, its location, and the overall size of the public relations department. Many firms offer benefits and compensation packages, including retirement plans, health and life insurance, or stock options that will further increase a manager's annual compensation.

WORK ENVIRONMENT

Public relations managers, especially those employed by large corporations, may have their own spacious office, or simply a desk in a cubicle, if at a smaller firm. Some high-level managers may enjoy benefits such as a company car, expense accounts, or access to free merchandise or services from different vendors.

The daily pace of a public relations office is usually busy and exciting, especially when workers are in the middle of an important publicity campaign, or when they are tackling multiple projects. Expect long hours—55- to 60-hour workweeks are the norm. Functions are often scheduled on evenings or weekends, which may affect a manager's personal or family time.

OUTLOOK

Employment for public relations managers is expected to grow faster than the average for all occupations through 2014, according to the U.S. Department of Labor. The high level of competition between certain businesses, especially those specializing in products and services, will create a demand for seasoned public relations specialists and managers to promote their companies as better than the rest.

Also, the Internet has had a global impact on business performance. Employers will look for candidates with superior computer skills and ease with Internet-based communication and promotions. Businesses that have international dealings may look for managers fluent in the language and customs of other countries.

FOR MORE INFORMATION

For a brochure on a career in management, contact
National Management Association
2210 Arbor Boulevard
Dayton, OH 45439-1506
Tel: 937-294-0421
Email: nma@nma1.org
http://nma1.org

For statistics, salary surveys, and information on accreditation and student membership, contact
Public Relations Society of America
33 Maiden Lane, 11th Floor
New York, NY 10038-5150
Tel: 212-460-1400
Email: prssa@prsa.org (student membership)
http://www.prsa.org

Public Relations Specialists

OVERVIEW

Public relations (PR) specialists develop and maintain programs that present a favorable public image for an individual or organization. They provide information to the target audience (generally, the public at large) about the client, its goals and accomplishments, and any further plans or projects that may be of public interest.

PR specialists may be employed by corporations, government agencies, nonprofit organizations—almost any type of organization. Many PR specialists hold positions in public relations consulting firms or work for advertising agencies. There are approximately 188,000 public relations specialists in the United States.

HISTORY

The first public relations counsel was a reporter named Ivy Ledbetter Lee, who in 1906 was named press representative for coal mine operators. Labor disputes were becoming a large concern of the operators, and they had run into problems because of their continual refusal to talk to the press and the hired miners. Lee convinced the mine operators to start responding to press questions and supply the press with information on the mine activities.

During and after World War II, the rapid advancement of communications techniques prompted firms to realize they needed professional help to ensure their messages were given proper public attention. Manufacturing firms that had turned their production facilities over

QUICK FACTS

School Subjects
Business
English
Journalism

Personal Skills
Communication/ideas
Leadership/management

Work Environment
Primarily indoors
One location with some travel

Minimum Education Level
Bachelor's degree

Salary Range
$26,870 to $45,020 to $84,300+

Certification or Licensing
Voluntary

Outlook
Faster than the average

DOT
165

GOE
11.09.03

NOC
5124

O*NET-SOC
11-2031.00, 27-3031.00

A public relations specialist prepares to address the press. *(Corbis)*

to the war effort returned to the manufacture of peacetime products and enlisted the aid of public relations professionals to forcefully bring products and the company name before the buying public.

Large business firms, labor unions, and service organizations, such as the American Red Cross, Boy Scouts of America, and the YMCA, began to recognize the value of establishing positive, healthy relationships with the public that they served and depended on for support. The need for effective public relations was often emphasized when circumstances beyond a company's or institution's control created unfavorable reaction from the public.

Public relations specialists must be experts at representing their clients before the media. The rapid growth of the public relations field since 1945 is testimony to the increased awareness in all industries of the need for professional attention to the proper use of media and the proper public relations approach to the many publics of a firm or an organization—customers, employees, stockholders, contributors, and competitors.

THE JOB

Public relations specialists are employed to do a variety of tasks. They may be employed primarily as *writers*, creating reports, news releases, and booklet texts. Others write speeches or create copy for radio, television, or film sequences. These workers often spend much of their time contacting the press, radio, and TV as well as magazines on behalf of the employer. Some PR specialists work more as *editors* than writers, fact-checking and rewriting employee publications, newsletters, shareholder reports, and other management communications.

Specialists may choose to concentrate in graphic design, using their background knowledge of art and layout for developing brochures, booklets, and photographic communications. Other PR workers handle special events, such as press parties, convention exhibits, open houses, or anniversary celebrations.

PR specialists must be alert to any and all company or institutional events that are newsworthy. They prepare news releases and direct them toward the proper media. Specialists working for manufacturers and retailers are concerned with efforts that will promote sales and create goodwill for the firm's products. They work closely with the marketing and sales departments in announcing new products, preparing displays, and attending occasional dealers' conventions.

A large firm may have a *director of public relations* who is a vice president of the company and in charge of a staff that includes writers, artists, researchers, and other specialists. Publicity for an individual or a small organization may involve many of the same areas of expertise but may be carried out by a few people or possibly even one person.

Many PR workers act as consultants (rather than staff) of a corporation, association, college, hospital, or other institution. These workers have the advantage of being able to operate independently, state opinions objectively, and work with more than one type of business or association.

PR specialists are called upon to work with the public opinion aspects of almost every corporate or institutional problem. These can range from the opening of a new manufacturing plant to a college's dormitory dedication to a merger or sale of a company.

Public relations professionals may specialize. *Lobbyists* try to persuade legislators and other office holders to pass laws favoring the interests of the firms or people they represent. *Fund-raising directors* develop and direct programs designed to raise funds for social welfare agencies and other nonprofit organizations.

Early in their careers, public relations specialists become accustomed to having others receive credit for their behind-the-scenes work. The speeches they draft will be delivered by company officers, the magazine articles they prepare may be credited to the president of the company, and they may be consulted to prepare the message to stockholders from the chairman of the board that appears in the annual report.

REQUIREMENTS

High School
While in high school, take courses in English, journalism, public speaking, humanities, and languages because public relations is based on effective communication with others. Courses such as these will develop your skills in written and oral communication as well as provide a better understanding of different fields and industries to be publicized.

Postsecondary Training
Most people employed in public relations have a college degree. Major fields of study most beneficial to developing the proper skills are public relations, English, and journalism. Some employers feel that majoring in the area in which the public relations person will eventually work is the best training. A knowledge of business administration is most helpful as is a native talent for selling. A graduate degree may be required for managerial positions. People with a bachelor's degree in public relations can find staff positions with either an organization or a public relations firm.

More than 200 colleges and about 100 graduate schools offer degree programs or special courses in public relations. In addition, many other colleges offer at least courses in the field. Public relations programs are sometimes administered by the journalism or communication departments of schools. In addition to courses in theory and techniques of public relations, interested individuals may study organization, management and administration, and practical applications and often specialize in areas such as business, government, and nonprofit organizations. Other preparation includes courses in creative writing, psychology, communications, advertising, and journalism.

Certification or Licensing
The Public Relations Society of America and the International Association of Business Communicators accredit public relations workers who have at least five years of experience in the field and pass a comprehensive examination. Such accreditation is a sign of competence in this field, although it is not a requirement for employment.

Other Requirements

Today's public relations specialist must be a businessperson first, both to understand how to perform successfully in business and to comprehend the needs and goals of the organization or client. Additionally, the public relations specialist needs to be a strong writer and speaker, with good interpersonal, leadership, and organizational skills.

EXPLORING

Almost any experience in working with other people will help you to develop strong interpersonal skills, which are crucial in public relations. The possibilities are almost endless. Summer work on a newspaper or trade paper or with a television station or film company may give insight into communications media. Working as a volunteer on a political campaign can help you to understand the ways in which people can be persuaded. Being selected as a page for the U.S. Congress or a state legislature will help you grasp the fundamentals of government processes. A job in retail will help you to understand some of the principles of product presentation. A teaching job will develop your organization and presentation skills. These are just some of the jobs that will let you explore areas of public relations.

EMPLOYERS

Public relations specialists hold about 188,000 jobs. Workers may be paid employees of the organization they represent or they may be part of a public relations firm that works for organizations on a contract basis. Others are involved in fund-raising or political campaigning. Public relations may be done for a corporation, retail business, service company, utility, association, nonprofit organization, or educational institution.

Most PR firms are located in large cities that are centers of communications. New York, Chicago, San Francisco, Los Angeles, and Washington, D.C., are good places to start a search for a public relations job. Nevertheless, there are many good opportunities in cities across the United States.

STARTING OUT

There is no clear-cut formula for getting a job in public relations. Individuals often enter the field after gaining preliminary experience in another occupation closely allied to the field, usually some segment of communications, and frequently, in journalism. Coming into public relations from newspaper work is still a recommended route. Another good method is to gain initial employment as a public relations trainee or intern, or as a clerk, secretary, or research assistant in a public relations department or a counseling firm.

ADVANCEMENT

In some large companies, an entry-level public relations specialist may start as a trainee in a formal training program for new employees. In others, new employees may expect to be assigned to work that has a minimum of responsibility. They may assemble clippings or do rewrites on material that has already been accepted. They may make posters or assist in conducting polls or surveys, or compile reports from data submitted by others.

As workers acquire experience, they are given more responsibility. They write news releases, direct polls or surveys, or advance to writing speeches for company officials. Progress may seem to be slow, because some skills take a long time to master.

Some advance in responsibility and salary in the same firm in which they started. Others find that the path to advancement is to accept a more attractive position in another firm.

The goal of many public relations specialists is to open an independent office or to join an established consulting firm. To start an independent office requires a large outlay of capital and an established reputation in the field. However, those who are successful in operating their own consulting firms probably attain the greatest financial success in the public relations field.

EARNINGS

Public relations specialists had median annual earnings of $45,020 in 2005, according to the U.S. Department of Labor. Salaries ranged from less than $26,870 to more than $84,300.

Many PR workers receive a range of fringe benefits from corporations and agencies employing them, including bonus/incentive compensation, stock options, profit sharing/pension plans/401 (k) programs, medical benefits, life insurance, financial planning, maternity/paternity leave, paid vacations, and family college tuition. Bonuses can range from 5 to 100 percent of base compensation and often are based on individual and/or company performance.

Top Employers of Public Relations Specialists, 2005

Employer	# Employed	Mean Annual Earnings
Advertising and related services	27,520	$57,160
Professional and similar organizations	15,050	$55,470
Colleges and universities	11,910	$44,420
Local government	8,670	$48,460
Management of companies and enterprises	7,570	$56,970
Federal government	3,870	$72,600

Source: U.S. Department of Labor

WORK ENVIRONMENT

Public relations specialists generally work in offices with adequate secretarial help, regular salary increases, and expense accounts. They are expected to make a good appearance in tasteful, conservative clothing. They must have social poise, and their conduct in their personal life is important to their firms or their clients. The public relations specialist may have to entertain business associates.

The PR specialist seldom works the conventional office hours for many weeks at a time; although the workweek may consist of 35 to 40 hours, these hours may be supplemented by evenings and even weekends when meetings must be attended and other special events covered. Time behind the desk may represent only a small part of the total working schedule. Travel is often an important and necessary part of the job.

The life of the PR worker is so greatly determined by the job that many consider this a disadvantage. Because the work is concerned with public opinion, it is often difficult to measure the results of performance and to sell the worth of a public relations program to an employer or client. Competition in the consulting field is keen, and if a firm loses an account, some of its personnel may be affected. The demands it makes for anonymity will be considered by some as one of the profession's less inviting aspects. Public relations involves much more hard work and a great deal less glamour than is popularly supposed.

OUTLOOK

Employment of public relations professionals is expected to grow faster than the average for all occupations through 2014, according to the U.S. Department of Labor. Competition will be keen for beginning jobs in public relations because so many job seekers are enticed by the perceived glamour and appeal of the field; those with both education and experience will have an advantage.

Most large companies have some sort of public relations resource, either through their own staff or through the use of a firm of consultants. They are expected to expand their public relations activities and create many new jobs. Many small companies are now hiring public relations specialists, adding to the demand for these workers. Additionally, as a result of recent corporate scandals, more public relations specialists will be hired to help improve the images of companies and regain the trust of the public.

FOR MORE INFORMATION

For information on accreditation, contact
International Association of Business Communicators
One Hallidie Plaza, Suite 600
San Francisco, CA 94102-2818
Tel: 415-544-4700
http://www.iabc.com

For statistics, salary surveys, and information on accreditation and student membership, contact
Public Relations Society of America
33 Maiden Lane, 11th Floor
New York, NY 10038-5150
Tel: 212-460-1400
Email: prssa@prsa.org (student membership)
http://www.prsa.org

——— INTERVIEW ———

Anne Unger is manager of system public relations for Resurrection Health Care in Chicago, Illinois. She discussed her career with the editors of Careers in Focus: Public Relations.

Q. Tell us about your work as a public relations manager.
A. I work in the corporate offices of the health care system, so my role involves any public relations effort or campaign that

includes the entire system (or most of it) of eight hospitals and other facilities. Sometimes I may help manage or support larger facility-based projects for the local public relations contact. I'm also involved with crisis-management issues at times since they are handled through the System Public Relations department.

I've been at Resurrection Health Care for a little more than two years, thus I've only been in crisis management for that length of time. I do, however, have more than five years experience in media relations and 11 years total in public relations.

Q. Why did you decide to enter the field of public relations?
A. Public relations is a dynamic field that offers a variety of roles and allows you to work with various people from laymen to executive levels, in all departments within an organization, and with people from other companies, including media, vendors, and other businesses. It's new and different every day.

Q. What are the three most important professional qualities for public relations specialists?
A. 1. Personable and diplomatic—being able to create, build, and foster relationships
2. Adaptable—staying open and willing to change with the demands of the role as often as necessary
3. Being a strong, honest communicator and storyteller through concise writing and articulate speaking

Q. What advice would you give to high school students who are interested in this career?
A. There is no better way to learn about the various areas of public relations than hands-on work experience. I would first recommend researching internship opportunities available to high school students. Internships are not just for college students anymore, and landing an internship while in high school will undoubtedly make a college application stand out—and help the student figure out if a public relations career is a good fit for him or her. If there aren't any companies offering high school internships in an area, students can contact the human resources department of companies they might be interested in working for with a resume and cover letter that includes their interests, what they hope to study in college, and how the internship would help advance their career aspirations. The same approach can be taken with small, non-for-profit organizations that operate on a shoestring budget and could never reject volunteers. The student would need to make sure

the role is clearly stated, however, so that responsibilities fall within the realm of public relations and other duties, such as handyman, are not added.

Q. What do you like most and least about public relations?
A. I most enjoy working with others in a collaborative effort to put together important news stories and working with news media to tell the story. It's a great feeling to see your efforts transcend your public relations role and become critical to the news media landscape.

One of the biggest challenges in the role of public relations is managing multiple projects and people, making sure your needs are understood and that you are not prevented from meeting deadlines or staying within a set budget.

Publicists

OVERVIEW

There are two types of *publicists*: those who work for companies, movie studios, recording companies, sports teams, and other organizations and those who work for individuals such as Chief Executive Officers, actors, musicians, and professional athletes. *Publicists* who are employed by companies and organizations handle the daily press operations for the organization. They handle media relations, arrange interviews, ensure that the correct information is distributed to the press, and write press releases. Those who work for individuals try to enhance their client's image by casting them in a positive light via newspaper, magazine, television, and Internet stories and other methods. Publicists are sometimes called *press agents, public relations (PR) directors, marketing directors,* or *directors of communication.*

HISTORY

Publicists have long been experts at influencing the public's perception of a business, organization, or individual. Using press releases, photographs, and other forms of media, publicists gain public recognition for their client. Publicists also take advantage of the popularity of the Internet by creating video news releases, e-mail press releases, e-mail invitations, polls, and surveys. The popularity of publications and Web sites, reality television shows, talk shows, entertainment programs, and countless cable channels covering the entertainment, sports, business, and other industries have provided publicists a huge outlet for media coverage.

THE JOB

Publicists are responsible for obtaining positive attention and name recognition for their clients. They achieve this by developing a publicity plan that may incorporate a variety of methods—press kits, news releases, photographs, personal appearances, and promotions. Using their many contacts and media savvy, publicists can turn a new restaurant or club into the latest hotspot, or reverse the fading career of a former A-list actor. Publicists may also be called to perform damage control—sometimes spinning a negative incident into a positive one, or at the very least, making a story less harmful to the client's reputation. A publicist's talents can be applied to many industries. The following paragraphs detail the many career options available to publicists.

Entertainment. In the entertainment industry, where being at the right parties and nightclubs can further an actor's public image and career, having a good publicist is an asset. Publicists promote actors and actresses by getting them invited to parties and premiers and involved in charity events and social causes that will make the individual more visible and attractive to the press and the public. They may schedule radio and television interviews, press junkets, personal appearances, television and radio interviews, and photo sessions to help promote an upcoming project. They often work closely with managers, agents, image consultants, and stylists to help the actor or actress portray a certain image that is favorable to the public. At times, a publicist may be called on to *spin* or interpret a negative incident into one less career damaging.

Sports. Publicists who work in the sports industry are responsible for the promotion of a team or athlete. They write press releases, hold press conferences, and arrange media interviews and tours. They often work with the public relations, advertising, and marketing departments of professional sports teams to create press releases, game programs, brochures, recruiting kits, media kits, and fan newsletters.

Publicists may also work to generate fan interest in a sports team or athlete by scheduling special events before, during, and after competitions; creating ticket or product promotions; and organizing music or fireworks displays.

Publishing. Publicists help promote an author's latest work by sending it to reporters, writers, and book reviewers employed at newspapers, trade papers, magazines, and Web sites. They may schedule and advertise a multicity book tour, including signings and reading at bookstores, schools, and libraries. Publicists may book an author, especially if he or she is well-known, for interviews and personal appearances on television and radio shows, as well as on the Internet. The may also promote the author's work for special awards and industry recognition.

Hospitality. The hospitality industry relies on publicists to promote its properties. Publicists employed in this industry often send press releases and media kits to travel magazines, travel agents, convention planners, and frequent guests of the hotel to create interest in the properties. Publicists may fine-tune or tailor media kits and other promotional material to attract a particular audience. For example, material sent to travel magazine editors would spotlight the hotel's unique spa services or nearby attractions; convention planners and travel agents would be sent highlights of the hotel's meeting facilities and guest rooms. Hospitality publicists also promote entertainment options found at hotels. A publicist employed by a Las Vegas hotel, for example, would tout its high-roller casinos, lounge acts and shows, or world-class dining. They might also showcase special events held at the hotel such as a New Year's Eve extravaganza or a slot machine tournament.

Restaurants. Besides delicious food and impeccable service, restaurants rely on good publicity to attract clientele. Publicists working in the restaurant industry need to promote their clients in a way that makes them stand out from the crowd. They work with restaurant owners to identify an appropriate image for the restaurant and the type of customers it wishes to attract—whether tourists, business people, young and hip urban professionals, families with children, or another demographic group. Publicists plan special events such as wine tastings, holiday theme parties, and fashion shows as a way to attract new diners to their establishment. These events may be listed in a calendar or flyer mailed or e-mailed to local media or frequent patrons. Publicists may invite the media to special events in hopes of garnering publicity in the form of a positive restaurant review or a mention in an upcoming column. Publicists may invite local television or radio personalities to do a live broadcast from the restaurant or bar to get additional publicity.

REQUIREMENTS

High School

As a publicist, you are the voice of the person or organization that you represent, so it is very important to be an effective communicator. Take classes in English, writing, and journalism to hone your writing skills, and take speech classes to help you learn how to compose your ideas and thoughts and convey them to an audience. You should also take other college preparatory classes, such as math, science, and foreign language. A general knowledge of history, sociology, psychology, and current events will also be useful.

Postsecondary Training

Most publicists are college graduates with degrees in public relations, marketing, communications, or journalism. A college degree is essential, according to the Public Relations Society of America.

Certification or Licensing

The Public Relations Society of America and the International Association of Business Communicators accredit public relations workers who have at least five years of experience in the field and pass a comprehensive examination. This certification will help show prospective employers that you possess a high level of knowledge and experience.

Other Requirements

In order to be a successful publicist, you should be outgoing and able to get along with many different types of people. You should also be creative, organized, and able to work well under stress, since you will likely interact with big-name clients.

EXPLORING

Ask your teacher or counselor to set up an information interview with a publicist. Volunteer to handle various public relations-type duties for your high school sports teams or clubs. Run for student council or another leadership position at school to gain experience with public speaking and management.

EMPLOYERS

Publicists work for public relations firms that handle publicity for companies, sports teams, and other organizations. Others work directly for companies. Some are self-employed, working directly with clients.

STARTING OUT

The best way to become a publicist is by gaining experience at the collegiate ranks. Many internships are available at this level, and landing one is the best way to get your foot in the door. As an intern, you may be asked to contribute to publications and write and prepare press releases. This will give you a great opportunity not only to learn how to generate all of this material, but also to begin collecting samples of your writing and to develop your clip file. Every interviewer you meet will ask you for your clip file, since it provides proof of your journalistic and public relations writing skills. Established public relations companies may also offer in-house training programs.

ADVANCEMENT

Publicists advance by gaining employment with more prestigious organizations, companies, or individuals, or by opening their own public relations firms. Others leave the field to teach public relations at colleges and universities.

EARNINGS

Publicists earn anywhere from $20,000 to more than $250,000 per year. Those just starting out might earn less, while those with proven track records command higher salaries. Publicists who work for individuals can earn higher salaries.

Most full-time positions provide life and medical insurance, pension, vacation, and holiday benefits.

WORK ENVIRONMENT

During busy times, publicists may work 12- to 20-hour days, seven days a week. Some publicists travel with their clients, while others do not. Either way, this job is very time-consuming.

OUTLOOK

The U.S. Department of Labor predicts that employment of public relations specialists in general is expected to increase faster than average for all occupations through 2014, but the number of applicants with degrees in the communications fields (journalism, public relations, and advertising) is expected to exceed the number of job openings.

FOR MORE INFORMATION

For information on working as an entertainment publicist, contact
Entertainment Publicists Professional Society
PO Box 5841
Beverly Hills, CA 90209-5841
Tel: 888-399-3777
Email: info@eppsonline.org
http://www.eppsonline.org

For information on accreditation, contact
International Association of Business Communicators
One Hallidie Plaza, Suite 600
San Francisco, CA 94102-2818
Tel: 415-544-4700
http://www.iabc.com

For information on careers and accreditation in public relations, contact
The Public Relations Society of America
33 Maiden Lane, 11th Floor
New York, NY 10038-5150
Tel: 212-460-1400
Email: prssa@prsa.org
http://www.prsa.org

━━━ INTERVIEW ━━━

Mona Loring is the owner of M. Loring Communications in West-lake Village, California. She discussed her career with the editors of Careers in Focus: Public Relations.

Q. Can you tell us about your business?
A. M. Loring Communications is a small public relations firm that services literary, small business, and entertainment industries. We are geared most toward literary and entertainment public relations, however. We have a staff of four, and we have been in business for one year.

Q. Why did you decide to enter this career?
A. I entered public relations because I always loved writing. I started out as a freelance journalist and ended up learning public relations at a small publisher in Malibu, California, that liked my writing style. After learning the ropes, I opened my own business.

Q. What do you like most and least about your job?
A. Most: I love that I deal with so many people on a daily basis. This job is definitely not boring. I also love that I get the chance to write each day.
  Least: There is a lot of pressure in this business. My clients count on me to get them results, so I cannot disappoint them if I want to succeed.

Q. What are the three most important professional qualities for success in this field?

A. 1. Communication skills. If you have difficulty communicating both written and verbally, you will not gain the respect you need from the editors and producers you deal with daily.

2. Determination. If you fail, you get right back up, figure out what you did wrong, and try it again. You cannot succeed unless you give it your all.

3. Confidence. You are in charge of selling someone or someone's product. If you don't have confidence in yourself, you will not have confidence in your client—or at least, it will seem that way.

Q. What is the future employment outlook in the field?

A. I truly believe that this is one profession that will always be around. Everyone needs someone to represent them. Although many other careers are perceived to die out in the future due to computers, robots, and technological advancements, public relations will always be around because the position cannot be replaced.

Webmasters

OVERVIEW

Webmasters design, implement, and maintain Web sites for corporations, educational institutions, not-for-profit organizations, government agencies, and other organizations. Webmasters should have working knowledge of network configurations, interface, graphic design, software development, business, writing, marketing, and project management. Because the function of a Webmaster encompasses so many different responsibilities, the position is often held by a team of individuals in a large organization.

HISTORY

The Internet developed from ARPANET, an experimental computer network established in the 1960s by the U.S. Department of Defense. By the late 1980s, the Internet was being used by many government and educational institutions.

The World Wide Web was the brainchild of physicist Tim Berners-Lee. Although Berners-Lee formed his idea of the Web in 1989, it was another four years before the first Web browser (Mosaic) made it possible for people to navigate the Web simply. Businesses quickly realized the commercial potential of the Web and soon developed their own Web sites.

No one person or organization is in charge of the Internet and what's on it. However, each Web site needs an individual, or team of workers, to gather, organize, and maintain online data. These specialists, called Webmasters, manage sites for businesses of all sizes, nonprofit organizations, schools, government agencies, and private individuals.

QUICK FACTS

School Subjects
Computer science
Mathematics

Personal Skills
Communication/ideas
Technical/scientific

Work Environment
Primarily indoors
Primarily one location

Minimum Education Level
Some postsecondary training

Salary Range
$45,427 to $66,975 to
$91,031+

Certification or Licensing
Voluntary

Outlook
Much faster than the average

DOT
030

GOE
11.01.01

NOC
2175

O*NET-SOC
N/A

THE JOB

Because the idea of designing and maintaining a Web site is relatively new, there is no complete, definitive job description for Webmasters. Many of their job responsibilities depend on the goals and
needs of the particular organization for which they work. There
are, however, some basic duties that are common to almost all
Webmasters.

Webmasters, specifically site managers, first secure space on
the Web for the site they are developing. This is done by contracting with an Internet service provider. The provider serves as
a sort of storage facility for the organization's online information, usually charging a set monthly fee for a specified amount
of megabyte space. The Webmaster may also be responsible for
establishing a uniform resource locator, or URL, for the Web
site he or she is developing. The URL serves as the site's online
"address" and must be registered with InterNIC, the Web URL
registration service.

The Webmaster is responsible for developing the actual Web site
for his or her organization. In some cases, this may involve actually
writing the text content of the pages. More commonly, however,
the Webmaster is given the text to be used and is merely responsible
for programming it in such a way that it can be displayed on a Web
page. In larger companies Webmasters specialize in content, adapta-
tion, and presentation of data.

In order for text to be displayed on a Web page, it must be format-
ted using hypertext markup language (HTML). HTML is a system
of coding text so that the computer that is "reading" it knows how
to display it. For example, text could be coded to be a certain size or
color or to be italicized or boldface. Paragraphs, line breaks, align-
ment, and margins are other examples of text attributes that must
be coded in HTML.

Although it is less and less common, some Webmasters code text
manually, by actually typing the various commands into the body of
the text. This method is time consuming, however, and mistakes are
easily made. More often, Webmasters use a software program that
automatically codes text. Some word processing programs, such as
WordPerfect, even offer HTML options.

Along with coding the text, the Webmaster must lay out the elements of the Web site in such a way that it is visually pleasing, well
organized, and easy to navigate. He or she may use various colors,
background patterns, images, tables, or charts. These graphic elements can come from image files already on the Web, software clip

art files, or images scanned into the computer with an electronic scanner. In some cases, when an organization is using the Web site to promote a special event or company community relations initiative, the Webmaster may work with a public relations specialist or department to develop a page.

Some Web sites have several directories or layers. That is, an organization may have several Web pages, organized in a sort of "tree," with its home page connected, via hypertext links, to other pages, which may in turn be linked to other pages. The Webmaster is responsible for organizing the pages in such a way that a visitor can easily browse through them and find what he or she is looking for. Such Webmasters are called *programmers* and *developers;* they are also responsible for creating Web tools and special Web functionality.

For Webmasters who work for organizations that have several different Web sites (for example, one site for business-to-business sales, one for the general public, and one that focuses on a particular community outreach initiative such as an annual literacy campaign), one responsibility may be making sure that the style or appearance of all the pages is the same. This is often referred to as *house style.* In large organizations, such as universities, where many different departments may be developing and maintaining their own pages, it is especially important that the Webmaster monitor these pages to ensure consistency and conformity to the organization's requirements. In almost every case, the Webmaster has the final authority for the content and appearance of his or her organization's Web site. He or she must carefully edit, proofread, and check the appearance of every page.

Besides designing and setting up Web sites, most Webmasters are charged with maintaining and updating existing sites. Most sites contain information that changes regularly. Some change daily or even hourly. Depending on his or her employer and the type of Web site, the Webmaster may spend a good deal of time updating and remodeling the page. He or she is also responsible for ensuring that the hyperlinks contained within the Web site lead to the sites they should. Since it is common for links to change or become obsolete, the Webmaster usually performs a link check every few weeks.

Other job duties vary, depending on the employer and the position. Most Webmasters are responsible for receiving and answering e-mail messages from visitors to the organization's Web site. Some Webmasters keep logs and create reports on when and how often their pages are visited and by whom. Depending on the company,

Web sites count anywhere from 300 to 1.4 billion visits, or hits, a month. Some create and maintain order or visitor response forms or online "shopping carts" that allow visitors to the Web site to purchase products or services. Some may train other employees on how to create or update Web pages. Finally, Webmasters may be responsible for developing and adhering to a budget for their departments.

REQUIREMENTS

High School

High school students who are interested in becoming a Webmaster should take as many computer science classes as they can. Mathematics classes are also helpful. Finally, because writing skills are important in this career, English classes are good choices.

Postsecondary Training

A number of community colleges, colleges, and universities offer classes and certificate and degree programs for Webmasters, but there is no standard educational path or requirement for becoming a Webmaster. While many have bachelor's degrees in computer science, information systems, or computer programming, liberal arts degrees, such as English, are not uncommon. There are also Webmasters who have degrees in engineering, mathematics, marketing, and public relations.

Certification or Licensing

There is strong debate within the industry regarding certification. Some, mostly corporate chief executive officers, favor certification. They view certification as a way to gauge an employee's skill and Web mastery expertise. Others argue, however, that it is nearly impossible to test knowledge of technology that is constantly changing and improving. Despite the split of opinion, Webmaster certification programs are available at many colleges, universities, and technical schools throughout the United States. Programs vary in length, anywhere from three weeks to nine months or more. Topics covered include client/server technology, Web development, programs, and software and hardware. The International Webmasters Association and World Organization of Webmasters also offer voluntary certification programs.

Should Webmasters be certified? Though it's currently not a prerequisite for employment, certification can only enhance a candidate's chance at landing a Webmaster position.

What most Webmasters have in common is a strong knowledge of computer technology. Most people who enter this field are already well-versed in computer operating systems, programming languages, computer graphics, and Internet standards. When considering candidates for the position of Webmaster, employers usually require at least two years of experience with Internet technologies. In some cases, employers require that candidates already have experience in designing and maintaining Web sites. It is, in fact, most common for someone to move into the position of Webmaster from another computer-related job in the same organization.

Other Requirements

Webmasters should be creative. It is important for a Web page to be well designed in order to attract attention. Good writing skills and an aptitude for public relations and marketing are also excellent qualities for anyone considering a career in Web site design.

EXPLORING

One of the easiest ways to learn about what a Webmaster does is to spend time surfing the World Wide Web. By examining a variety of Web sites to see how they look and operate, you can begin to get a feel for what goes into a home page.

An even better way to explore this career is to design your own personal Web page. Many Internet servers offer their users the option of designing and maintaining a personal Web page for a very low fee. A personal page can contain virtually anything that you want to include, from snapshots of friends, to audio files of your favorite music, to hypertext links to other favorite sites, to information promoting a community service project in which you have participated.

EMPLOYERS

The majority of Webmasters working today are full-time employees, according to *Interactive Week*. They are employed by Web design companies, businesses, corporations, public relations and advertising firms, schools or universities, not-for-profit organizations, government agencies—in short, any organization that requires a presence on the World Wide Web. Webmasters may also work as freelancers or operate their own Web design businesses.

STARTING OUT

Most people become Webmasters by moving into the position from another computer-related position within the same company. Since most large organizations already use computers for various functions, they may employ a person or several people to serve as computer specialists. If these organizations decide to develop their own Web sites, they frequently assign the task to one of these employees who are already experienced with the computer system. Often, the person who ultimately becomes an organization's Webmaster at first just takes on the job in addition to his or her other, already established duties.

Another way that individuals find jobs in this field is through online postings of job openings. Many companies post Webmaster position openings online because the candidates they hope to attract are very likely to use the Internet for a job search. Therefore, the prospective Webmaster should use the World Wide Web to check job-related newsgroups. He or she might also use a Web search engine to locate openings.

ADVANCEMENT

Experienced Webmasters employed by a large organization may be able to advance to the position of *online producer.* These workers supervise a team of Webmasters and are responsible for every aspect of a company's presence on the Web. Others might advance by starting their own business, designing Web sites on a contract basis for several clients rather than working exclusively for one organization.

Opportunities for Webmasters of the future are endless due to the continuing development of online technology. As understanding and use of the World Wide Web increase, there may be new or expanded job duties in the future for individuals with expertise in this field.

EARNINGS

According to Salary.com, the average salary for Webmasters in 2007 was $66,975. Salaries ranged from less than $45,427 to more than $91,031. However, many Webmasters move into the position from another position within their company or have taken on the task in addition to other duties. These employees are often paid approximately the same salary they were already making.

According to the National Association of Colleges and Employers, the starting salary for graduates with a bachelor's degree in computer science was $50,820 in 2005. Those with a bachelor's degree in information sciences and systems received average starting salary offers of $44,775.

Depending on the organization for which they work, Webmasters may receive a benefits package in addition to salary. A typical benefits package would include paid vacations and holidays, medical insurance, and perhaps a pension plan.

WORK ENVIRONMENT

Although much of the Webmaster's day may be spent alone, it is nonetheless important that he or she be able to communicate and work well with others. Depending on the organization for which he or she works, the Webmaster may have periodic meetings with graphic designers, marketing specialists, online producers, writers, public relations specialists and managers, or other professionals who have input into Web site development. In many larger organizations, there is a team of Webmasters rather than just one. Although each team member works alone on his or her own specific duties, the members may meet frequently to discuss and coordinate their activities.

Because technology changes so rapidly, this job is constantly evolving. Webmasters must spend time reading and learning about new developments in online communication. They may be continually working with new computer software or hardware. Their actual job responsibilities may even change, as the capabilities of both the organization and the World Wide Web itself expand. It is important that these employees be flexible and willing to learn and grow with the technology that drives their work.

Because they don't deal with the general public, most Webmasters are allowed to wear fairly casual attire and to work in a relaxed atmosphere. In most cases, the job calls for standard working hours, although there may be times when overtime is required.

OUTLOOK

According to the U.S. Department of Labor, the field of computer and data processing services is projected to be among the fastest growing industries for the next decade. As a result, the employment rate of Webmasters and other computer specialists is expected to grow much faster than the average rate for all occupations through 2014. As more and more businesses, not-for-profit organizations, educational institutions, and government agencies choose to "go online," the total number of Web sites will grow, as will the need for experts to design them. Companies are starting to view as important and necessary business, marketing, and public relations tools.

One thing to keep in mind, however, is that when technology advances extremely rapidly, it tends to make old methods of doing things obsolete. If current trends continue, the responsibilities of the Webmaster will be carried out by a group or department instead of a single employee, in order to keep up with the demands of the position. It is possible that in the next few years, changes in technology will make the Web sites we are now familiar with a thing of the past. Another possibility is that, like desktop publishing, user-friendly software programs will make Web site design so easy and efficient that it no longer requires an expert to do it well. Webmasters who are concerned with job security should be willing to continue learning and using the very latest developments in technology, so that they are prepared to move into the future of online communication, whatever it may be.

FOR MORE INFORMATION

For information on training and certification programs, contact the following organizations

International Webmasters Association
119 East Union Street, Suite F
Pasadena, CA 91103-3952
Tel: 626-449-3709
http://www.iwanet.org

World Organization of Webmasters
9580 Oak Avenue Parkway, Suite 7-177
Folsom, CA 95630-1888
Tel: 916-989-2933
Email: info@joinwow.org
http://www.joinwow.org

Index